Karl Gutzkow

Through Night to Light

Karl Gutzkow

Through Night to Light

ISBN/EAN: 9783744752725

Printed in Europe, USA, Canada, Australia, Japan

Cover: Foto ©ninafisch / pixelio.de

More available books at **www.hansebooks.com**

COLLECTION
OF
GERMAN AUTHORS.
VOL. 16.

THROUGH NIGHT TO LIGHT BY K. GUTZKOW.

IN ONE VOLUME.

THROUGH NIGHT TO LIGHT.

BY

KARL GUTZKOW.

FROM THE GERMAN
BY
MRS. FABER.

Authorized Edition.

LEIPZIG 1870
BERNHARD-TAUCHNITZ.

LONDON: SAMPSON LOW, MARSTON, SEARLE & RIVINGTON.
CROWN BUILDINGS, 188, FLEET STREET.
PARIS: C. REINWALD & C¹ᵉ, 15, RUE DES SAINTS PÈRES.

CONTENTS.

		Page
CHAPTER I.	The House with the Sign of the "Flying Horse"	1
— II.	Grandfather Mordaunt in Ipswich Street	11
— III.	Passages in "Little Lobster's" Life	22
— IV.	The future Lord Chancellor of England	43
— V.	The Bracelet	63
— VI.	Joyful Anticipations	99
— VII.	Will Mordaunt keeps his Word	130
— VIII.	The French Enchantress	181
— IX.	The Death of the Queen	225
— X.	The Judge's Sentence	258

THROUGH NIGHT TO LIGHT.

CHAPTER I.

The House with the Sign of the "Flying Horse"

"By George! Who are you slandering? Two angels live in that house."

"By St. Patrick, I will confess that is true of one, but as for the other it is a demon; its claws—"

"Who, what? Do you mean the Papist? Your countryman? You may perhaps be right—"

"Papist! Ha ha? And at the same time one of the king's murderers! He believes in nothing; he is never to be seen in church."

"Well, well. He certainly prays, but only to his money-bags. Them he fills, hum—hum. Strange things are said about that."

"St! He must be a coiner."

"Who? My neighbour yonder? That little man? He is the best-hearted fellow in the world; a benefactor to the poor; no one knocks at his door in vain."

Thus, over a draught of brisk ale, were different opinions broached respecting a London citizen, in one of the numerous taverns which surrounded his house. It was about the year 1713, rather before than after, and at the time when, in a brilliant apartment of the castle in Hanover, the German Elector, George Louis, was making immediate preparations for embarking, at one of his small harbours, in the North Sea, to take possession of the sceptre of Great Britain, already almost as powerful as the trident of Neptune. This sceptre at present rested in the hands of a woman whose life was ebbing away, his near relation, Queen Anne.

The White Flying Horse, the cognizance of the House of Guelph, was also the sign of the house inhabited by the man upon whom these different judgments were passed. With him it took its origin from the horse-market, which in old times was held at the upper part of Lincoln's Inn Fields.

The business world knew with greater certainty than the world of tavern-frequenters that John Robertson, so the proprietor of the house was called, had been living some years ago in poverty although he was of no mean descent, and had made a good marriage. Shortly after his marriage, so it was said, Mr. Robertson ceased to make his payments, and many were most bitter in their reproaches, because they said that, in order to increase his own fortune, he had gained the confidence of a respectable family solely that with his wife's money he might either pay off some early debts hitherto unacknowledged, or be able to enter more boldly into speculations, with which he was gambling away his existence. Others, who professed to be better informed, denied the truth of these assertions and called John Robertson a miser, who after his marriage with Mary Wilson, the daughter of a country clergyman with whom he had become acquainted on one of his business journeys, had compelled his young wife to live with him in poverty, whilst he hoarded savings upon savings, and had at length become a very rich man. But then again they reflected that after a long period of poverty John Robertson showed the world that his means were increasing, and denied his wife no kind of pleasure, which however in consequence of an early death she did not long enjoy. Thus, this reproach of stinginess did not prove valid, and beyond the precincts of the taverns people became accustomed to regard John Robertson as a man of property and surrounded by strange mysteries, one whom the world must simply take as he chose it they should.

This little grey-haired man, who was always courteous to all his neighbours lived, as is customary in London, in a separate house. The house was his own; it was not large, but with its little balconies, big windows, with their small panes of glass, and its spiral staircase, it was very old-fashioned but very convenient. In accordance with the notions of comfort and luxury of those days, the three stories of the house were all connected by a staircase, which was covered with rich carpet to deaden the sound of footsteps.

John Robertson's establishment was not large. During the time of his difficulties he had acquired the habit of waiting almost entirely upon himself. His surroundings were therefore a little peculiar. He could not endure that anyone should stay near him long. None of his acquaintance were particularly intimate with him. He himself lived on the ground-floor and kept all the keys of the house in his own possession. If a loud knock was heard at the house-door, he not unfrequently opened it himself. Every night, he extinguished all the lamps in the house, with his own hands; and these eccentricities served to increase the strange rumours and reports which were current about him. It was said that in the day-time he would shut himself up for hours, without anyone being able to guess what he was doing. Then again it was said that as strange noises were often heard in his room at night, it might be supposed likely that he slept in the day. Those who lived in the house never saw him leave his bedroom before eleven o'clock in the morning. It was not until this hour that he required the simple soup flavoured with ginger and vegetables which in those days formed the early breakfast. He was always the last person up at night, for he required of his servants that they should be in bed by eleven at the latest. It was believed that he then sat up till midnight or after, or perhaps (but in this opinions were divided) quitted the house altogether or received visits from unknown and mysterious men. No one was admitted to any close intimacy with this strange John Robertson, except an old tradesman living in a suburb on this side of London. This dirty and in every respect unpleasing man was called Will Mordaunt.

John Robertson kept up the closest friendship with him; and it must be confessed that this intimacy contributed not a little to increase the reports about Robertson; and to make him often appear in a light not favourable to his character. For, from the old horse-market still surrounded by little gardens to the most distant streets in the city, it was known of Master Mordaunt that he acted as a pawnbroker, lent money on usury, sold inferior goods at a high price, undertook commissions of every kind as, for instance, the hiring of servants from whom he took payment;

in short Will Mordaunt passed for one of the meanest of misers, not only in Ipswich Street where he lived, but also throughout the whole of that side of London between Ipswich Street and Islington. To see courteous, smiling Mr. Robertson, who was alwas handsomely and well dressed, with his buckled shoes and even his sword, allowing this man to come in and out; to know that they were closeted together, and even counting money, and all this throughout the space of long years, was so astonishing that Mr. Robertson had no right to be surprised; when, although people could not deny him the name of a humane, benevolent and conscientious man, they held aloof from him, and avoided any nearer intercourse whenever the little man appeared to seek for it.

For it was one of John Robertson's more respecable characteristics that up to a certain point he was noted for hospitality. Mysterious as were his nights and mornings, often in the middle of the day he felt it a necessity to unlock the doors of his house and to admit, as in the old times of his early happiness, whoever might wish or like to come in. Many were heartily glad to come; his table was excellent; his wine received the approbation of the best judges. The difficulty was in calling afterwards When his guests wished to pay their friendly host a morning visit, he was always either asleep or not at home. The curtains were drawn and the whole house, was dead, at least in the front where the Flying White Horse was above the entrance.

John Robertson had one daughter named Ellinor, a lovely, charming creature. It was to please her that her father gave parties.

Robertson had married when about six and thirty; and this child born in the ninth or tenth year of his marriage with good, much-tried Mary Wilson was the only one of his otherwise childless marriage. As her mother died a few weeks after her birth, her father had himself brought up and educated the child. In her infancy, while little Ellinor was still fed with the milk of a cow bought expressly for her and kept in the immediate vicinity of their no longer humble abode, her father had passed even the nights, which it appeared so indispensable he should spend in solitude, in exclusive devotion to his child; in carrying her in his arms and guarding her like the apple of his eye, as the last legacy of love which his wife had bequeathed to him with a smile in her dying moments. The inquisitive censors of his mysterious life began to say Mr. Robertson will soon cease to prosper, if he has to take care of his child at night instead of coining bad gunieas. Others declared he would be obliged to marry again for that he would never allow the strangers who would have to assist in the education of his child to obtain an insight into his mysterious mode of life. However the solitary widower took care of his child himself. But, when she grew older and became stronger, he gave her up at night entirely into the charge of a housekeeper, who was made to sleep on the third floor of his house, and she was often changed. The father himself superintended the education of his child; he was tormented by his impatience to see Ellinor grow into a blooming, well-grown girl. Even before she could spread out her little fingers he wished to seat her at the most perfect spinnet that could be obtained in London; and to have her instructed by masters who gave lessons in the fashionable world. In those days, people in England, depreciating what belonged to home, began to imitate everything foreign and especially French; and gave a preference to French customs and language. Thus Robertson adopted this language and made use of it in his daily intercourse with his child. He took part in all the child's exercises, was present at all the lessons given by the masters, and fortunately had time for it. He lived half his life in the night; the remainder of it was spent in dreaming by daylight. To enter again into business would have disturbed the calm of his life;

would have troubled the stillness of his home. Will Mordaunt repeatedly asked him to enter into joint undertakings with him. But close as the intimacy between these two men appeared to be, Robertson had little liking for the principles of his friend as regarded trade. Whatever surplus he had he put into the East India Company's bank; they gave good interest. Half of this he was again enabled to invest as capital which he was saving for Ellinor. But he had other sources of income. Whence these were derived was a secret even from his child. Ellinor grew up until sixteen in happy unconcern on all these subjects, was the joy and pride of her father, and never suspected that she was destined to be the cause of his greatest grief.

It was a delicious spring such as may be enjoyed even in London, at least in the little garden of such a house as the Flying Horse. The buds of reviving nature were bursting; the garden shears of that period, conspicuous for want of taste, had already begun to cut and chop the hedges just beginning to change their brown for green, and the budding crowns of the still leafless trees, but they could not destroy all the blossoms in the hidden corners covered with violets, at the back of the house. Ellinor rejoiced over every flower which she put into the pretty little vase of exquisite china lately invented and placed in her own room. An elder bush with its numerous, half-opened, purple buds already covered a high wall which led to another street, Wenlock Street. Yet this lovely season was destined to be the beginning of a severance in life which would cause heavy clouds to gather over John Robertson's long untroubled sky of happiness.

CHAPTER II.

Grandfather Mordaunt in Ipswich Street.

WE have already said that Will Mordaunt was John Robertson's sole and confidential friend in matters of business. But it would be even more correct to say that Mordaunt appeared to exercise a sort of dominion over Robertson, so much so that one might almost say he had the little man under his thumb. Robertson, at least, was not at all astonished when, one day on which he had left his small but comfortable house, the "Flying Horse", the front of which looked out into Cavendish Street, and had taken a walk to Islington and called on Will Mordaunt, this pawnbroker and seller of second-hand clothes expressed himself thus in the intervals of his hectic cough:

"My good old friend, it is only of late that I have been willing to think of dying, but my two boys, Tom and Sam, compel me to meditate on life and death. You know that their father left them no legacy but my affection as their grandfather. I have hoarded and hoarded in order to make, as I have done, gentlemen of my grandsons who will scarcely be able in future to greet me, when, in the company of their well-bred companions from Eton and Oxford, they meet their old grandfather in the street. But the ties of blood cannot be neglected, and——as the laws of England prescribe that I should provide for Tom better and more largely than for his younger brother Sam, for the sake of these old customs which have made England great, and which, please Heaven, will make her greater still in spite of priestcraft and French intrigues, I, and in this case, for my own sake also am.——"

John Robertson understood his intentions very well. He gave a clap on the shoulder to the old miser whose eyes were buried in his pock-marked face like "two little pieces of butter in a dish of stewed peas," according to the expression of his grandson Sam, and said with a consciousness that what he said would be agreeable to the pride of Will Mordaunt and to the great desire of his life,

"Friend, I still recall with pleasure how I held two fine children at the baptismal font. Let your humility stand reproved and be assured, I perceive that you are anxious to celebrate your eightieth birthday in no less a manner than by having the Bishop of Winchester's coach stop at your house. Would that I myself might but live to see Tom thus elevated."

The grandfather of Tom and Sam Mordaunt did not in the least combat the possibility of such a future for his grandson Tom, although the latter was as yet only invested with the dignity of a vicar. He might already have added to his lamentation, the information that Tom had succeeded in touching the heart of a young lady of position. The solemn tone of his present conversation arose from news which the old man had received of the impending engagement of his eldest grandson to the daughter of one of the most wealthy aldermen at Pemford in Pemfordshire, an engagement the fulfilment of which was only delayed by one condition, that the future inheritance of that excellent young man Thomas Mordaunt should be clearly defined, and a settlement made according to the wishes of the rigid and exacting parents of his betrothed, the Alderman of Pemford and his wife.

Master Will, the grandfather, was therefore resolved to bequeath his own considerable fortune to his son's first-born according to English custom, without any condition in favour of the younger child, provided that what had indeed long been a darling wish of the Master of the damp, dark rooms of the ruined house in Ipswich Street should be fulfilled.

This was none other than that the fortune of his

younger grandson should be founded by his old friend and the boy's godfather John Robertson.

Robertson's fortune was superior to that of his friend. Will Mordaunt had had one son whom an imprudent marriage had brought to the verge of a complete breach with his father (who would not allow himself to be imposed upon) as well as to the shortening of his own life. He died young, deeply involved in debts, the payment of which took the larger portion of Mordaunt's income. Indeed, the very line of business of this latter, was exposed to the danger of having, after great winnings, to expect equally large losses, yet his property was sufficiently considerable for the future Bishop of Winchester, or at least for levelling the steps of the ladder for him up to a deanery, he being already a vicar. For Samuel Mordaunt, the younger grandson, on the contrary, a learned, adventurous, extravagant boy, and certainly no enemy to money, for this no less beloved grandson, Sam, the old pawnbroker and usurer had for many years thought of the hand of Ellinor Robertson, as the best provision. Her hand, and why not? A seat in parliament, and, at the very least, the portfolio of an under secretary of state, if not the seals of the Lord Chancellor himself, not to be procured perhaps under Queen Anne who was still reigning, but certainly under her successor, in case, (and here the old English patriot laughed as at something evident to himself) the succession to the throne, should, by the grace of Heaven, remain in the protestant royal family now secluded in Hanover, and not pass to the accursed Catholic Stuarts who were wandering about in the world.

In former times Ellinor's father had been tolerably well inclined to agree to this plan. Often before his pretty Ellinor was born he had said to his friend,

"Old Will, if you and your two grandsons did not make such faces, which renders them both as ugly as you are yourself, then if I had no children I would adopt them, provided they had not too much of your greed for gold, and did not inherit as a family characteristic your want of cleanliness."

But now he himself had a daughter, and the two Mordaunts had with years improved in appearance. Indeed Sam had that characteristic ugliness which under some circumstances, especially when a man has expressive eyes and plenty of talent, proves really attractive.

Ellinor was well acquainted with her father's godchildren; she had so to speak lived with them as companions from her earliest youth. Sam was one of the few men whom she saw frequently. The only male acquaintances of her early years had been her father, "Little Lobster" (as she had jestingly named him when she was a child, because he was generally dressed in red), an old servant now dead, Cab the milkman who himself brought the cow's milk with which she was nourished, the newspaper carrier, and Will Mordaunt, who gave her an idea that all men of wealth and importance were marked with the small-pox, (this last also, Sam Mordaunt was, according to the unfortunate fate of those times when inoculation was still unknown). Thomas Mordaunt, the eldest grandson, was further removed from her in age. And now that she had for some little time gone out more into the great world, "Little Lobster" knew very well what sharks and other fish of prey were likely to swim after his dear child in that large sea. Manners, at that time, in London were very loose and bad, in consequence of the ever-increasing imitation of the French, so that careful fathers found it doubly necessary to take good care of their daughters. Sam Mordaunt, the lawyer, had almost vanished from the north side of London for the last few years, and had only returned for flying visits, even from Eton or the University. As the friend of youthful lords, perhaps he was ashamed of the dirt of Ipswich Street. Ellinor had always been accustomed to compare the men of whom she heard or read with Sam. Those on whom the hopes of father or grandfather rested had always in her imagination sparkling black eyes; teeth of dazzling whiteness; thick, black hair beneath the curled wig; a sword at their side and a peculiar smile such as, to say the truth, was always playing round Sam's lips. The pock-marks did not disturb her. Sam had grown up so unlike anyone but himself, so attractive and at the same time so repulsive, that Ellinor could well understand, how in thinking of those who do not belong to their own family, women always have occasion to feel more fear than joy. But this idea in no way prevented her from always being glad at heart when Sam Mordaunt paid her a visit, either as a school-boy, or from Oxford, or as a young lawyer at the Temple.

Indeed, the older Sam and Ellinor grew, the more strange was the proportion between the throbbings of her heart when he was expected, and the steps with which he bounded up to the third floor of her house. For instance, the older she became the quicker her heart beat, while Sam, on the contrary, mounted the stairs more slowly, and now for a full year he had been particularly thoughtful during his visits. Papa Robertson had much fault to find with him. He blamed him that after his three years spent in learning different branches of the law, and even after a journey to Paris for improvement, he should again return to the University. Further, he blamed him for often looking morose or offended and angry; again, because he talked little, was absent and wandering in mind, and, in, fact was no longer like his former self. Then Ellinor defended him. And thus, on this beautiful May morning, when the churchyards clad in their spring dress had enticed him to Islington (his dear Mary lay in the churchyard of St. Paul, already removed far into the suburbs) the "Little Lobster" was fully justified in saying off hand to the grandfather, "Only cure your frightful cough, by friend, and everything else will go well. Ellinor knows her father very well. She can do what she likes with me; we often dispute but never seriously. She will from her heart say "Yes" to your boy, if only he himself wishes to hear this little word, which decides the fate of life, said in church."

"You don't say so?" replied Mordaunt.

It is true that he felt flattered by this disclosure, yet it annoyed him for several reasons. For he had suffered enough from the pride of his grandson, which this latter, as he used to say, must have inherited from his mother, the daughter-in-law who had cost himself so many sleepless nights, so much money, and at length the untimely death of his only son, who perhaps—hum—this supposition he was accustomed to crush in the bud,—might have done better for himself. Both the old men agreed in this, that Sam thought too little of those who would have desired to press him most closely to their hearts.

But in all this Will made excuses for him; "He is obliged to make up to great people; it cannot be otherwise if a man wishes to make his way in the world as a lawyer. Read this letter, Sir, it is just as I said. Tom, who not only was bent on being a clergyman but much to his injury really is one, was wicked enough to lose his temper (Heaven forgive him!) when Sam called him names for wishing to curtail his inheritance on account of his own marriage with a goose from Pemford—she has indeed much too long a neck, though it is very white—and for not agreeing to an arrangement for a yearly income but asking immediately for his portion which should be paid when I shall lie under the turf at St. Luke's or St. Giles'. But there is no help for it. As I could not do otherwise than go to Mr. Cracksby, (he meant the lawyer) and also could not do otherwise than arrange my will as they insisted upon at Pemford before they would sanction the engagement, Sam is prepared from this day forward to open his shop, and to hang up a signboard with the inscription (ha! ha! this is what he writes) "Here the gallows are robbed of their prey!" In short, he establishes himself as a lawyer, and what he thinks of your Ellinor, godfather, you may read for yourself. In my opinion they will make a good, excellent, pious pair."

Godfather John read the abominable scrawl of the young lawyer who was now, as he wrote, travelling in Scotland, and intended afterwards to return to London (this was the plan) and to bring for Ellinor all the strawberries which he had seen blossoming in the Northumberland woods and on the banks of the Tyne. He desired his kindest remembrances to her, and called her a turtle-dove, because he had heard that she wished to learn to sing though she had not yet succeeded. And this was just as well, especially if she were to be a simple, pretty dove.

The father read this sentence in a voice of mingled joy and melancholy, and promised that the sweet hopes intimated by Sam, who had just reached his five-and-twentieth year, with regard to Ellinor, who was scarcely yet sixteen, should be fulfilled, and that on this very day he would tell his beloved child of her future destiny.

Further discussion on this important question was prevented by old Mordaunt's business. He was again wanted for a negociation, and on this occasion it related to the transport of a number of Methodists who intended to emigrate to Pennsylvania, out of fear, as was said, of a credible prediction immediately to be fulfilled, of the certain and universal reinstatement of the Catholic faith in England.

These people purchased of him two whole roomsfull of old clothes. With the simple words, "There on folio 7852 is your present balance", Will Mordaunt turned to the two pious men who wished to ascend with him into the old-clothes room.

John Robertson turned to page 7852, muttered "Two guineas, eleven shillings", gave a sigh which seemed expressive of a weight at his heart, and betook himself thoughtfully and not without some anxiety to his quiet home in Cavendish Street, to announce to his child that she was shortly to be betrothed to the young Mr. Samuel Mordaunt, and to marry him within a year. With regard to his child's obedience to this order he had no anxiety, but he felt more than ever a certain oppression with regard to the position in which he stood with Will Mordaunt of Ipswich Street. Perhaps he felt vexed that the future Lord Chancellor of England, as Sam sometimes called himself in his letters, should have called him not "Little Lobster" but "Marmot." He felt that this might very well be a play upon his strangely long hours of sleep which he sometimes prolonged until nearly noon.

CHAPTER III.

Passages in "Little Lobster's" Life.

CERTAINLY old Robertson's manner of walking was most peculiar; he always looked down upon the ground. Many people said that it was his shy consciousness that prevented him from looking straight before him, but when they pointed the finger at him and thought to meet in him the personification of an uneasy conscience, they themselves had reason to look on the ground ashamed. For at such moments the old man would often raise his bowed head and look up with an expression of innocence that was almost childlike, and bright as the sunshine of a summer day. Then their cocked-hats were taken off and they bowed till the peaks almost touched the pavement. Men greeted each other with more formality in the year 1713 than they do now-a-days.

We have already said that Mr. Robertson's house was in Cavendish Street, in a district which at that time was quiet both on Sundays and on week-days, and in which the houses had little gardens at the back, and had even a view of sundry old lime-trees. From his house a building stretched out to the small garden, which was surrounded by a high wall. He had no need to traverse this garden when he wished to leave his house secretly and did not care to make use of the door over which the Flying Horse was enthroned (a railway runs past it now), for in this building there was a little door, which was always kept locked, leading into Wenlock Street, a much more lively street and one in which bustle was going on till late at night. In this street, where a philosopher might pace reflectively up and down unobserved and be only occasionally a little jostled, John Robertson strode back and forwards some hundred paces in vain; then he stood still, then turned again, till at length he took courage and went down Cavendish Street.

He resolved to give Ellinor an account of his conversation with Will Mordaunt.

All went better than he had promised himself. Ellinor readily reconciled herself to the prospects which her father held out of her future destiny. He began at first to talk of the rapid course of time, of the uneasy doings in the great world, of life and death as regarded men in general, of the emigrants to Pennsylvania and specially of certain old Quaker hats; then he passed on to Mordaunt's unhealthy, even dropsical appearance; his short breath in ascending the stairs and the break-neck ladder leading to his stores of old clothes. Then he spoke of Thomas Mordaunt's marriage and described the situation of Pemford in Pemfordshire, and the pride of the little town, which owed its origin to a certain kind of delicious cheese; till at length he arrived at Sam Mordaunt's legal sign with its inscription which was in no way contrary to the manners of those times, "Here jail-birds accounts are settled." Ellinor laughed heartily.

Her father next began, "But no, I will see to it that he does not announce himself to be a protector of criminals. These lawyers now-a-days will almost ogle at the iron bars in Newgate! Anyone who has a murder on his conscience is like some rare plant from the Indies. Then they study how to describe everything about the little bush that grows in the botanical garden of humankind (alas! a garden of well-developed wickedness) and link all together. No, he should rather make his sign a token to lovers, poor betrothed couples who are tormented by their parents or relations, and are unable to obtain from them permission to accomplish their wishes. If he would become reconciled to his brother the vicar and obtain a good and honourable position in society, he might write upon his sign what I have already seen in Bow Street and read in the neighbourhood, "Here people may be married well and for ever."

Ellinor laughed merrily and looked so pretty at this moment that in gazing at her her father forgot the thread of his discourse. But various thoughts came into his mind. First of all, he was struck with the contrast between Sam Mordaunt and Ellinor; the one was a man of ungoverned nature, a complete tiger; the other a girl, timid and gentle as a dove. He looked at his child with emotion. How pretty she was as she sat before him in the high, well-cushioned arm-chair of Indian wood inlaid with mother-of-pearl! The sun, which in London is no frequent guest, but which when it did shine, had free entrance into Ellinor's room on two sides, fell straight on the rosy cheeks of his little daughter, which glowed more than usual in the expectation of what it might be that her father appeared to have to tell her.

Ellinor had soft blue eyes and fair hair which curled naturally. On this day it was dressed in an unusual manner like a coronet formed of little curls. A string of amber was twined among her ringlets and confined them. Gold on gold? the fashionable young lady of modern days will ask. But at that time fashions were not so much of a science, and that which now appears wanting in taste still had a pleasing effect. To the yellow of her hair and yellow of the amber was also added a yellow silk dress. It was so heavy that when she sat down it swelled out stiffly round her. "My golden child," "my little canary-bird" she might well have been called by her father when in this dress. Even the shoes on her little feet and their high heels were all yellow. This was about the year 1713. In our day Ellinor's graceful figure of about the middle height, her fair hair, her complexion of milk and roses, as it used often to be called, would have been adorned in quite a different manner and fashion. One may imagine her room with its old Chinese mandarins; its clock which at every hour made a rumbling noise intended to represent a graceful melody; its large mirror set in golden garlands and a number of artificial flowers in japanned vases. On the table lay some prayer-books and some books of travels in Japan and Ceylon. In a warm corner stood a spinnet with black keys and tones so thin, oh! as thin as threads of silk if one can compare sound with anything visible. The text to the notes was French.

One wall was entirely covered with a mirror; on the other hung pictures of the brave Tamerlane and proud Zenobia, in ornamented bronze frames, intended to represent garlands of flowers. These were the principal characters played in the pieces at that time in the theatre which Ellinor, alas! was not often able to visit. Not that "Little Lobster" was by any means troubled by English scruples. No, it was only his own disinclination for the Haymarket, where a preference was given to Mongolian and Assyrian battles; to Covent Garden where the Italian singers sang; to Drury Lane where at that time Shakspeare was still a great unknown, immured and buried like Herculaneum or Pompeii. Pantomimes from the Netherlands had there a greater run than any other branch of the dramatic art.

Thus it happened that Ellinor was not very unwilling to agree to the disposal of her hand to Sam Mordaunt, because she hoped by this means to obtain some of her favourite wishes more quickly. She had so much longed for an Indian bird, a parrot. Down on the banks of the Thames, near the Docks, lived vendors of cocoa-nuts, tropical fruits, monkeys and parrots. Ellinor's lately engaged companion, Miss Kitty, had spent some time in Paris, (she was a genuine English girl from Yorkshire, but through various circumstances had found opportunity to learn how to dress in Paris)—in Paris, we say, Miss Kitty had seen that every lady of quality had a monkey with her. Ellinor, however, longed for a bird which should converse with her if she taught it to talk.

Perhaps also she was attracted by the idea that

if she were married she would be able very often to give orders that she should be carried to the Strand, alight there, and amid the throng occupied in bargaining for and buying all sorts of things, seek for a little Bab (for her feathered favourite must go by no other name,) and feel herself thoroughly free and able to join merrily in the bustle of the world. For she knew very well and had noticed it among many of the company collected (not without some difficulty) by her father, that it is a very convenient thing to be engaged, if only to enable one to breathe the fresh air occasionally. Then what would she not gain? When one has an arm at hand on which to lean, one need not always be carried in a sedan-chair or driven straight to the corner of the second street by the old coachman, Master Twistle, who was indeed a regular old grumbler.

But imagine! the purchase of a Bab was to take place on this very day independently of the engagement to be arranged between Ellinor and Sam Mordaunt. The fair girl in the course of the conversation about the advantages of this engagement, about Sam's eminent talent, and his excellent acquaintances, exclaimed,

"Papa, now I must go to the Haymarket and see Colley Cibber in his beautiful comedy 'She will and she will not.'"

This was a fashionable piece of the day. But the father broke in on this fancy with the following words,

"I see, my child, that you are an obedient daughter in everything, true inheritrix of all the good qualities of your mother, which good qualities, if I could estimate them in gold, would come up to the mark of fifteen or sixteen carats. Nearer to perfection no one can approach. Some copper, some gold, some human ingredients such as are called temperament, flesh and blood and the disposition we naturally inherit render inevitable; otherwise, whilst on earth we should already be angels, such as my good Mary became, all too soon, in another world. You place me in the (to me) very agreeable position of being able to remove from old Cerberus in Ipswich Street all anxiety about his younger grandson, the future Lord Chancellor of England. I pray Heaven that I may never repent my trust in your obedience; still more that you may never repent, my dear child. But as for going to the Haymarket of which you talk, well, well, you had better go there with Sam; I cannot go to these theatres."

At these words an expression passed over his face, not of religious disinclination, but of alarm; and a slight shudder seemed to shake the old man from his very shoulders. That he should almost immediately knit his white eyebrows, was only because the natural outbreak of noise and joy which the announcement of an approaching betrothal is wont to produce, found vent even in the quiet house of John Robertson in a running up and down stairs, a banging of doors, talking and laughing. The people most interested were Miss Kitty, Jane the cook whom Ellinor generally called "Pudding Jane" (because she prepared this favourite food of the English nation better than the former cooks who, according to her father's domestic system, had been frequently changed); Bob the man-servant, and Abram the messenger, who was only occupied in the house during the day and slept out. In addition there was an accidental witness, Cab the newsman, who (in a century when the influence of the press was only in its infancy, and was exercised cautiously amid many conflicts with the officers of the law, whose duty it was unceasingly to burn periodicals and journals) played a more important part than do in the present day our newsboys in the beer-shops, who offer their newest edition fifty times before they sell one. It was strange that Mr. Robertson bought everything which appeared at that time, in the form of pamphlets or weekly papers, and, what was still more strange, he always read the last sheet of the paper first, "the sheets where the advertisements are" as Miss Kitty used to say, who had only of late been admitted into the house, and who was immediately initiated into the strange traditions respecting the "Flying Horse," by the other servants and neighbours.

Now, amid the joy and bustle of sympathy and congratulations on the impending change in the house, Miss Kitty advised visits to all the public places of amusement. It was only natural to show oneself in the world. The publication of the banns in church was not sufficient to make people in general acquainted with such an event; the banns were only published a short time before the celebration of the marriage, the prospect of which was by no means at present so near. The old gentleman ought to show himself a little in London now! There were now circus-riders, dancers and singers to be seen, and nothing could be more proper than to appear surrounded by one's own family (Kitty was bold enough to include herself in this mathematical figure) at cockfights, dog and rat fights, and, at any rate, at the Haymarket and Drury Lane, and to take care to be in the front seat so that all the world might feel an interest in the merry laugh of the young girl, and in her enjoyment of the great box of bonbons which would be bought for her by her companion. Thus one announced to the world that it was not money which was riveting this tie, but a true and very hearty attachment. Miss Kitty maintained that she herself had borrowed her French tournure from the Parisian theatres; indeed she even repeated, in English however, some heart-breaking tirades from pieces which she pretended to have seen in Versailles, and took it very ill when old Robertson, who, for an Englishman, spoke French very well, declared that he could recognize all the peculiarities of the Yorkshire dialect in her pronunciation of those very passages in which she repeated scraps of French in her best style.

When the father was left alone again with his child (for Miss Kitty was in duty bound to go down to the underground floor to help the cook, especially in the preparation of that excellent dish which alone the old gentleman really appreciated), the most necessary thing that presented itself was to gratify Ellinor's longing for a parrot, and to select a new and rich dress appropriate to a more or less festive celebration of her betrothal. For the performance of both these commissions a sedan was necessary. These were invariably ordered from a letter-out of chairs who lived near by, (Mr. Pifferton, a reliable man) to the continual displeasure and vexation of the coachman Twistle who unfortunately was always standing with crossed arms at his house-door when instead of his horses two sturdy Welshmen endowed with herculean shoulders carried Mr. Robertson or his daughter to take the air. But Mr. Robertson felt more happy in trusting his daughter to these Welshmen than to Master Twistle's spirited horses. They would carry her to the grandest shops in Holborn and through the most riotous crowds in the Strand without a hair of her head being hurt.

With a smiling face and grateful heart she now said, "Be sure, dear father, that I no longer wish to go to Drury Lane or the Haymarket since I perceive that going to the theatre gives you so much anxiety about the safety of my soul."

"Oh! I am not troubled about the safety of your soul," replied her father; "that is safe enough even though you should see 'She will and she will not' and have a hearty laugh with Mr. Colley Cibber. No," he continued, but the thread of his discourse was suddenly broken by a glance which he had cast at the latest "Mercury," a London paper small as a dwarf by a giant in comparison with the modern "Times." He murmured a few words to himself, then looked up, cast a long, pleased glance at his beloved child and proceeded without showing any token of disquietude.

"On this day on which you have given me so sweet a proof of your filial obedience I may tell you why I have a horror of all theatres. Not that I hate them, since within their walls so many stories from life and proofs of the eternal control of Divine justice are represented which to some may afford instruction, though to others, who are unable to appreciate such feeling, it be only a play. But even they very often are obliged to take a hint of something good from words spoken in jest. No, the sight of these theatres awakes horror in my mind owing to the most fearful remembrance of my life. Not even your mother's death is to me so sad a memory. On the contrary we must all die, and to know that your mother is already above and preparing a place for my reception, that—"

"Father," said Ellinor, interrupting him affectionately.

"Yes," said the old man, the current of his thoughts taking a different turn. "But that was assuredly a fearful hour in which I lost the document that was to make your mother and me happy."

The only document that suggested itself to Ellinor under the circumstances as that which was to make a couple happy was the contract of betrothal. She interrupted him with the question,

"Was it before your marriage?"

"No, my child," replied her father in a communicative spirit not usual to him." On this day he indulged in it in consequence of the festive occasion which could only come once in his life. "No; our marriage would indeed hardly have taken place if the events of this fearful evening had happened before it."

Ellinor was all attention and now heard that her mother, Mary Wilson (who, as she was already aware, was the daughter of a country clergyman) had had an immensely rich relation who dreaded death and studiously avoided everything which suggested the idea of death. He was an old bachelor and was compelled by circumstances to make a will. Not that he was urged to do so by his relations, who on his death would as his natural heirs have better prospects than if old Uncle Buck should make a will and should, as often happens, take this opportunity of leaving his property and personal goods to pious institutions such as schools and hospitals. This in truth had been his intention, only he had never been able to summon resolution to look thoughts of death straight in the face. Indeed he had an especial dread of being left without aid or assistance in his last hours, if he should not leave his money to those who flattered him with outward love and as his well-pleased heirs. Some wonderfully worldly-wise man must have invented the laws of inheritance. Sometimes the aunt has a right to inherit and the cousin has not, or the cousin has and the aunt has not. This, as Ellinor's father explained to her, arises from the degrees of relationship. Mary Wilson would inherit nothing unless Uncle Buck chose. He did choose; for of all his relations the little daughter of the Northamptonshire clergyman was by far the dearest. Mary's father, he certainly did not like. As a clergyman he appeared much too black and solemn, reminding him of death whenever he met him. But the little girl continually brought fruit and flowers to him in his grand house where indeed he had abundance of both, but none that were brought with the words "Dear Uncle" or offered with a kiss on his tough, worn cheeks. When Mary was betrothed ("Yes, Ellie," said Ellinor's father, "this day recalls it vividly to my mind") Uncle Buck promised the young pair to make them a present of three thousand pounds. At his death the money was to be paid to them. The legacy was signed with his name. Any court of law must have acknowledged the deed. And on the strength of this paper, which in consequence of the seventy years of life to which their benefactor had attained must shortly be expected to be changed into three thousand pounds of hard cash, John Robertson had not indeed married (for he was a young merchant who had been by no means unsuccessful in forming a business in materials for ship-building), but in the prospect of this money he had embarked in important undertakings and in large speculations and purchases. The physicians assured them that Uncle Buck might die any day. Robertson's business friends thought the same and in expectation of such near and certain prospects did not press him. And indeed the old Uncle did die soon. The "smiling heirs" immediately took possession of everything and were not a little horrorstruck when they were informed that they were under compulsion to give up three thousand pounds to young John Robertson and his wife. But this deed which was of such extreme importance, which his lawyer conjured him never to allow to go out of his possession, which as soon as legal proceedings were instituted John Robertson always carried in his breast and fingered and felt a hundred times when he had to go to Doctors' Commons where it was acknowledged as a preliminary to be an evidence of the wishes of the testator, this paper was lost by the young pair at Drucy Lane Theatre just before the decisive day when the opposing parties were to appear before the judge.

Ellinor found herself suddenly awakened from her dreams when she perceived the powerful effect which the remembrance of this terrible occurrence had upon her father even at the present time. It was true that he endeavoured to soften the picture. He even laughed and said,

"It was a just punishment to us for having turned the season of mourning for a relation, who had desired our happiness, into a time of pleasure-taking."

Ellinor now understood why her father was always wont to sigh so deeply when he spoke of the season of sudden poverty which had overtaken him almost immediately upon his marriage. And now since on this day she had, as it were, come of age and become ripe for the discussion of the graver questions of life, she asked him,

"But could not the evidence of those who had already seen the document speak for the rights of my poor mother?"

"No indeed, my child," replied her father, smiling aside at the innocent and natural observation of so youthful and unsuspicious a disposition; "No, my child, the verdict depended on the so-called experts in the court of justice in Northampton. They had to examine the handwriting, to compare it with other undoubted specimens of our Uncle's own writing and to confute the accusation of forgery which had been maliciously raised. But the document was wanting! Our oaths, our assurances, nothing had any weight. How did I seek, seek, seek! Oh, my child, for three days and three nights a half-crazy man was to be seen rushing about everywhere through Drury Lane, Bow Street, Long Acre, Tavistock Street, with his eyes always down on the ground, hunting behind the pillars of every portico, asking everyone he met whether they had found a sheet of paper with some writing on it. I placed criers at the corners of the streets and promised rewards to whoever should bring back a document which was of no use to anyone but the owner, and which was mere waste paper to everyone except Mary Wilson now Mary Robertson. Yes, Ellinor, this it was which first stabbed your mother to the heart! For I was obliged immediately to close my office. I had made purchases on credit which I should not now be able to redeem. I was a ruined man and all this for the sake of a play, for the sake of a fashionable piece which Lord Lansdowne had written under the title of 'No magic like Love!' Yes, yes, Ellinor, this proved true with your mother and me; Love had made us blind. In paying for the tickets of admission, in the crowd of people, in the throng of handsome carriages, in the wild November storm which blew my hat off so that I was obliged to run to recover it (Ah! we were still then merry heirs), amid all this the fatal paper fell from my breast-pocket! Amid the rush in the theatre I did not discover my loss during the whole evening. I only saw the full house, only heard the play, the songs, laughed at the dancing and was delighted above everything with your mother's joy. Yes indeed, 'No magic like Love.' But on our return home we discovered our misfortune. Certainly when I immediately rushed back to the scarce yet emptied theatre and ran about among the people to discover my paper which had been wrapped in a piece of thin leather, they might well have believed that I had just escaped from Bedlam."

Ellinor perceived how great was her father's excitement, even in recalling these events. She tried to turn his mind to other thoughts. She pointed to that day's "Mercury" and said,

"Oh dear, oh dear, alas! In comparison with this the grief of Lady—what is she called—is but a mere joke."

This expression was intelligible to her father. He had already read on the last page of the Mercury (in which descriptions of articles lost and found were given) that a lady of the highest rank in St. James' had experienced the loss of a bracelet.

Meantime Miss Kitty had come in again; heard of Lady Arabella Ratcliffe's misfortune and said,

"I knew this noble lady very well in Paris where I often saw her at the house of our gracious Queen's Ambassador, Lord Stair; I know the ambassador's cook, for I was within a hair's-breadth of marrying him. But how so exalted a lady could have lost a gold bracelet studded with pearls in the poorest and dirtiest part of London, that I can not understand." Miss had taken the paper herself and wished to show that she too could read. "It must have been that one of her servants had orders to carry the costly trinket to a jeweller and that on his way to Dowgate he strayed into a public-house."

John Robertson bowed in his own peculiar manner, almost bending his ears down to the side of the speaker. He appeared to think her explanation by no means improbable; improved upon the conjecture of the wise young lady and sought, by representing the servant of Lady Arabella as probably engaged in love errands, to restore the former cheerfulness.

"No magic like Love," said he laughing and humming an air which he remembered from the play of his younger years.

Lord Lansdowne, the aristocratic author of these mixed dramas composed of spoken parts, of music, dancing and machinery, was still alive. According to the taste of those times he did homage to the fashion which Shakspeare had already seen coming in, and to which he himself with his last work "The Tempest," made his bow and then withdrew entirely from the stage. Lord Lansdowne had changed

Shakspeare's "Merchant of Venice" into "The Jew of Venice" and had made of it a lively comedy adding song and dance. All London was delighted with the modern Shylock because outside the most select and educated circles the genuine, old Shylock was no longer known.

Mr. Pipperton's sedan-chair had now arrived; Bob the house-servant announced it. The affectionate father accompanied Ellinor to the house-door. She ordered herself to be taken to Cornhill, that she might buy a handsome Lyons' dress, and to the Docks in order that she might purchase a gay Brazilian bird.

But her father remained at home and read with attention how things were going on in the outside world. The subjects which interested him the most were the condition of England, the parliamentary reports and numerous passages regarding the relations of France with the Stuarts or referring to the Elector of Hanover. But in a pocket-book he made a note of the name of Lady Arabella Ratcliffe.

CHAPTER IV.

The future Lord Chancellor of England.

It was a rainy November day, when a string of carriages accompanied by horsemen in strange attire, entered the gate from Islington on the north-west of London.

Everyone knew what this procession was. It consisted of students, bachelors of arts; who, having studied for a term of years, some till they were quite venerable, at Oxford or Cambridge, were making their entrance into London after the manner of students in those days, wishing to make it a public event. The ancient, mediæval spirit which even in the present day exists in England in so many of the relations of life, could not yet comprehend the modern mode of thought that the individual must be lost in the mass and only speak as expressing the wishes and hopes of the many. The procession of Lord Mayor's day had not altered the least in character. It exists to the present day as the outward token of consciousness of freedom among the citizens. But these processions of students have been given up in England.

The entrance through the gate at Islington of the monkeys, dogs, burlesque decorations of persons, carriages and horses, was on this day thoroughly watery, owing to the miserable state of the weather. The young men who numbered from ten to twelve (for the women among them were only men in disguise, and the artistically-made beards of the men might well have been natural if in those days fashion had tolerated hair on the chin and lips) made great efforts by shouts, singing and cracking of whips to testify their indifference to the floods of rain which, flowing down from the roofs of their half-open carriages, drenched their clothes through and through. But the riders with their plumed cocked-hats who tried to flank the carriages, made an even more miserable appearance by their transformation into "drowned rats", as one of the riders expressed himself, who allowed his a long sword to peep out from beneath his capacious cloak like the chief of a Highland clan.

In Bridgewater Square they made a halt. Here, beaten hither and thither by the storm, and amid the shrill tones of their leader, they entered into a council and came to the conclusion, that the endeavour to traverse the whole town, to scandalize all the inhabitants of the city and the customers in the Crown and Anchor Tavern, and only to disperse on the banks of the Thames in the Strand would be productive of no special success, and, therefore, each one would do best to endeavour to take refuge in house and home, either in his own carriage or on his own horse.

At that time more liberty prevailed in the streets of London than the citizens, and especially the Whig party, liked. England had attained the grandest success in battle; she had humbled France and Spain, both by sea and land. Queen Anne, the sickly daughter of James II., could point to this fame and to the proper generosity of a conqueror, when people complained of her mode of government and especially of her behaviour to the Tories and Catholic Stuarts. Her ministers were Tories, secretly followers of her half-brother, the Pretender, who was living in France and whom she secretly encouraged in his hopes of the succession to the throne, whilst the parliament and people had decided in favour of her sister's husband, the Elector George Lewis of Hanover. The waves of party feeling rose higher and higher as the moment drew nearer in which the queen must die.

When the procession had dispersed with a last salvo, expressive of all the follies which have place in the minds of youth even when most intellectual and sensible, with shouts, songs, imitations of the noises made by animals, and when its individual members had parted with mutual promises of reassembling at the place which had been fixed upon, one of the participators in the tumult turned back over a part of the road they had already traversed, then bent his steps northwards and came into one of the most confined and populous quarters of the city, that in which Ipswich Street was situated.

He had quitted a carriage, in which a young man still remained, who promised to bring all his luggage safely to the "well-known place" and who took leave of him with these words,

"Do not be late; boiling water will be good for us to-day."

By boiling water, however, he did not mean tea, but water mixed with gin.

The figure which strode with firm tread over the muddy streets (despising one of the eight hundred vehicles for hire which, we can assure our readers, were already established in London) was a tall, broad-shouldered man. His face was concealed by a cloak of red cloth with a high collar and innumerable capes, falling one over the other, such as our coachmen still wear. His plumed hat was pressed down over his eyes, which only peered out from beneath it just so much as was necessary to enable him to see his way, and to avoid running up against the people in the crowd. But for all this, the drenched man looked at every woman whom he met. If she were old (and it was always necessary to cast some glances of inquiry before his wraps and the fog would enable him to discern her age and appearance) then he muttered student like, "Gorgon." But if she were young then he said, "Angel," aloud, yet always pursued his way, indifferent when some antique affronted beauty called after him, "If you do not wish to grow old, scapegrace, you had better get hung while you are young!"

Further, when we say that our Oxonian son of the muses, who had attained to young manhood and was making his way to Ipswich Street, had a face that was marked with the small-pox, very keen black eyes, a turned-up nose and a protruding chin, the reader will easily recognize in him Samuel Mordaunt. Long ago Doctor of Laws and "Author on stamped paper," as he called himself, he still retained his student's manners. In spite of his betrothal he had allowed spring, summer and autumn to pass before coming to greet his charming *fiancée*. Now he found his grandfather bedridden. The Pennsylvanian emigrants had kept Will Mordaunt too long in a draught, among his stores of old clothes; for on account of the moths, these old clothes were always hung out at the open windows. In addition, his grandfather had been very much tried by the negociations with Alderman Pemford in

Pemfordshire and with his grandson Thomas, vicar of that place, so famous for its cheese. The deed conveying his whole property to the eldest of his grandsons was executed under the auspices of Lawyer Cracksby; and the concluding words, "Now farewell, old gentleman!" from the three men, the lawyer, the alderman and his own grandson Thomas, sounded almost as if they meant to say, "Now, old fellow, you cannot do anything better than travel for our benefit into another world." This too had done his health no good.

"It is certain that the fair hand of the beautiful Ellinor is destined for you. Then you may blame yourself if you dissipate money and possessions, and if you think to squander the fruit of hard work.

Thus did old Will groan out a greeting to his grandson from his bed which to a close observer was one of peculiar construction. It was exceedingly high and the bedding was made of down from the Shetland Islands where the wild goose is found. Under the bedstead was a large chest clamped with iron, to which was attached a little chain, which at night, when he went to bed, old Will made fast to his night-dress. Having already been robbed several times, and that cleverly by those greatest rogues in the world, London thieves, he had adopted this clever contrivance for being awakened immediately that any attempt should be made on his coffers. Besides, the room in which he slept was also his dwelling-room. His ledgers and all that he had he kept in this one place. The house was very old. The ceilings were composed of beams crossing each other. In former times they had probably been covered over with stucco, but now insects had been disporting themselves there and had eaten it away. At night the cankerworm sawed away the wood. But the old house still afforded shelter from wind and weather, and the only cause for fear was from the fires, which sometimes in London burnt down large portions of the town. This would have been a great misfortune, for Will Mordaunt had stores of every description. Much of his furniture bore traces even of taste and luxury. These had been articles which had come to him in the way of business and which, not indeed without a severe struggle, he had at length permitted himself to use.

Wilkie, a half imbecile and at the same time very deaf old man, was Mordaunt's factotum. He now helped the grandson to take off his wet clothes and brought dry ones almost as good as new from the stores above. This was certainly much to the displeasure of the sick man, who felt in no way disinclined to quarrel with the grandson, whom he blamed for the bad weather as though it were a personal injury and blamed also for slyly obtaining an outfit which he gave grudgingly.

"How to rule the weather, grandfather?" replied Sam. "No, Justinian does not teach us that! But you are right! In old times, when Duns Scotus and Albertus Magnus flourished, this also was taught at the universities; but then in order to manage it, people must need enter into a compact with the devil. That, however, is not my way, grandfather. I am a good Christian; although just now uncommonly hungry and thirsty. Will you order them to bring me something to eat and drink? I would rather have two mugsful than one, provided the old woman yonder adds too many onions to her cutlets as usual."

Sam Mordaunt devoured with appetite all that Wilkie brought in obedience to the look of the grandfather, and the latter gave him the money for it after diving for some time into his money-bag under the bed. It was dinner-time. Even in Ipswich Street people might at twelve o'clock have a tolerable meal from a cook-shop, established for workmen who had no homes of their own, and which provided board and lodging for artizans, and was often one of the numerous hells upon earth.

The old man who only indulged in water gruel,

and who was vexed at this affair of the clothes, returned to the topic of the weather and said,

"Yes, it is very strange and approaches almost to devilment that whatever the weather may be, whether dusty or rainy, you always come to my house in clothes which you leave behind you as remembrances, that you may take away with you others and better which I never see again."

"As remembrances? The clothes which I have taken off to-day I shall carry away with me, grandfather," replied Sam, trying to draw Will Mordaunt's attention to their excellence. But the old man persisted in calling the thick red cloak a coat which might have belonged to the Oxford hangman. He looked with anger at the black velvet coat slashed with gold, which Sam had just put on and which fitted his handsome figure as exactly as though it had been made for him. Under it, he had a white waistcoat with mother-of-pearl buttons, which reached almost to his hips.

"I hope that you now are intending to call upon your bride and to kiss the fair hand for which I have been obliged to entreat in your stead. To stay away six months afterwards! You will be well received! Give your promise at once that you will become a barrister of repute, and will put a respectable sign-board to your house and will try to get into parliament. Why are you always going about with your rollicking friends? Why do you expect me to drain my heart's blood in order to make you a favourite with young men, when they will not do the smallest thing to bring you into the 'Triennial;' (by this he meant the Parliament, the elections for which at that time took place every three years); must they be paid specially for it?"

Samuel tried to calm the old man. The thought of his betrothal with the little lady in the pretty, quiet house in Cavendish Street was ever vividly before him. He had indeed been brought up formerly to call his little playmate, Ellinor Robertson, his wife, yet the realization of this, which was depicted to him as a strange, invaluable, highly esteemed happiness, appeared to excite in him some powerful inward emotion, which even this cold and refractory young man could not prevent himself from betraying. With a bitter laugh and showing his white, well-set teeth by a contortion of his features, which appeared almost inhuman, he said,

"If I were only sure that in entering the family at the "Flying Horse," I should not also marry the rope still growing somewhere in the fields, which is destined to hang my father-in-law!"

His grandfather turned round in his bed, indignant at this rudeness. The chain of the chest rattled. So often as his grandsons (they had not lived in his house for long and had never been entrusted with the interior management of his business) had reminded him of the mysterious sources of old Robertson's wealth and of Mr. John's strange practices, as, for instance, his nocturnal expeditions, he had always answered them either angrily or jocosely, according to his mood. When in a good temper, he would confess that it was possible that the respectable old man with his white hair might be a coiner, that he might possibly clip the coin of the realm and might even be on friendly terms with thieves and murderers. But everyone knew for certain that this was not so. When, however, he was in a bad humour he preferred not answering at all. On this occasion a cold shudder passed over him when Sam, nothing daunted by the presence of deaf Wilkie, to whom it was necessary to shout if one meant him to hear, said,

"I should very much like to find out all that is carried on in Mr. John's cellar, outbuildings and other premises, and why there is that little arched doorway into Wenlock Street."

Silence pervaded the room. Outside, the midday chimes were sounding; carriages were rattling along the street; they could hardly hear themselves speak for the noise. When this had ceased in a degree and old Mordaunt had recovered from a fit of coughing, which seemed to shake the whole of his powerfully-made frame, Samuel explained that he was intending to stay with a nephew of Lord Nairn's, Lord Arthur Maxwell, a young Scotchman, who was already anxiously expecting him and to whose house his luggage had been taken. Thither old Wilkie was also to bring the handsome clothes he had just taken off.

Will Mordaunt laughed bitterly and muttered some words which might have been as follows,

"He will not even leave me his old rags as a compensation."

As Sam thought he perceived that Wilkie did not proceed sufficiently carefully with his wardrobe, to which he wished that respect should be paid, he himself seized upon the basket in which his clothes were to be carried to Lord Nairn's, and was going to arrange them.

Wilkie had just gone down into the shop to send out one of the shop-boys (of whom many were actively employed besides the two book-keepers of this carefully conducted and flourishing business) with orders to fetch a hackney coach, that Mr. Sam might first of all make his visit to Ellinor Robertson with dry feet.

When Samuel opened the large basket before

packing his clothes, he perceived at the bottom of it a hard substance, wrapped up in a piece of paper.

His grandfather heard the rustling, seemed immediately to revive and half raised himself hurriedly from his bed of pain. It was gout which tormented him even more than his cough, and sometimes caused him to utter grievous groans.

"What is this?" cried Sam in astonishment, when he had unfolded the paper; "a gold bracelet!"

His grandfather already had one foot out of bed, but as the bed was very high he could not so quickly reach the ground. He propped his gouty foot on the stool, which served to aid him to mount into bed.

"Holloa, what is it?" he cried; "it is nothing for you."

"What do I see?" said Sam, with an expression of increasing astonishment. "This costly trinket has on it the initials of a name which I know!— B. C."

His lips remained motionless; the first initial he, muttering between his teeth, interpreted as Blanche. The second name which was represented by the letter C, died on his half-opened lips.

"Where did this come from? It has been stolen from a lady whom I know."

"Stolen!" said the old man, mimicking the voice of his grandson, in which astonishment and indignation were mingled; "do you intend to take it to the Old Bailey and there earn for yourself the character of a pettifogging lawyer?"

"How did you come by this costly ornament? It is worth at least forty guineas."

Taking advantage of the surprise of his grandson, the old man had already snatched away the bracelet. Notwithstanding his pain and his anger, he presented a laughable appearance. His long stockings, his gown with the girdle to which at night the chain of his chest of gold was made fast, his night-cap, the point of which fell down over his face which had become white with alarm, all these escaped the notice of the grandson, who at all events appeared to regard this valuable ornament as a precious booty for himself.

"The thing was advertised in the Mercury and cried as lost, and Wilkie was smart enough to find it. He will claim the reward, although any shop in Smithfield would give him fivefold the amount of the so-called 'handsome' reward which the lady—what's her name?—the paper is lying there—has promised to bestow."

Already before his grandfather had finished making this explanation to the still greatly troubled

Samuel, the latter had found the Mercury on the window-sill, had opened it and turned hastily to the place where the advertisements were. He did not perceive that it was a very old number.

"At Lady Arabella Ratcliffe's in Grosvenor Square," said he, shaking his head which glowed all over, and listening to the old man who again drew himself into his bed and grasped the bracelet closely.

"It must have been lost in Lambeth Street. Yes! who knows what roundabout way the scoundrel of a servant took, who ought to have carried it to the goldsmith. Here at the clasp there is a link loose and it would very soon have broken entirely. Where did you find it, Wilkie?" continued the old man, addressing the servant, who was coming up the stairs at the moment and whose hearing was completely destroyed by the rattling of the carriage close by. "That gold thing I mean, Bob," he cried. "Did you not go down Lambeth Street or somewhere in that direction the evening before last, when you were a little the worse for the gin you had been taking, old stupid?"

Will Mordaunt did not speak these last words altogether with the sharp intonation, which it is usual to use in addressing a deaf person, but rather in the tone of a man who suggests to another the answer which it is desired he should make to the question asked him.

Bob Wilkie was not the man to diverge by many words of his own from that which his patron and benefactor of many years wished should be corroborated, nor did he indulge in a protest against the predilection for gin so frequently attributed to him; neither did he enter into a lively description of how it had happened, that between ten and eleven o'clock on the evening before last he had stumbled upon a thing, which he at first took for a brass ring that might have fallen from a sedan-chair or from the harness of some horse (Will Mordaunt gave all these graphic and minute details), how on picking it up he had been astonished and had brought it here to Samuel Mordaunt's grandfather, acknowledged to be so respectable an appraiser of such articles and a diligent reader of the Mercury. Wilkie contented himself with nodding three times and saying, "In Budge Road." He then respectfully announced that the coach was below and that Sam would have to pay for the time he might keep it waiting.

When Samuel repeated "In Budge Road! How comes B. C.?"—then Bob Wilkie began to talk of an old house with an overhanging first story, of an arched door not far from the Sailor-boy Tavern, and the grandfather looked at the clock which ticked near him and called out, "The hackney coach! These minutes are costing you sixpence."

At these words he clutched the bracelet still more firmly as though the fingers of his right hand had been of iron. Bob Wilkie's grasp was equally powerful. The place whither he was to carry the basket of clothes was, so to speak, equally firmly rivetted in the grasp of his memory. Now for the sixth time Sam described to him where the young Lord Maxwell lived. To look again at the bracelet, to contemplate the initials B. C. twined together and surmounted by a coronet, was a thing not to be thought of by the grandson. His grandfather prevented all that. For, as has already been said, this was not the first time that the young student, who had just come from Oxford, had looked on objects of a similar kind as booty, and had made them vanish out of his grandfather's sight for weeks and months. Samuel's bold spirit, always ready to act, and to carry out what he resolved upon without any troublesome prickings of conscience, was on this occasion prevented from noticing a similar dishonesty about the bracelet by his astonishment and his reflections as to how the lady, denoted by the initials B. C. (for when she was in London she could only be staying at Lady Arabella Ratcliffe's) should have entered the precincts of Budge Road and even of the Sailor-boy. That she was in London he had already half suspected.

His further inquiries were very much restricted by the necessity in which he found himself of asking his grandfather for considerable sums of money for his expenses in London, and for many debts which he had contracted in Oxford.

"This is the last," said the old man as he put his hand into his cash-box, which stood in an old oak cupboard, which could only be opened by a curiously-made key hanging on a large bunch of keys, and evidently debating whether he should take more or less; "this is the last money I will give you. I do not choose that your brother, although he is a clergyman, should rail at me. I have cleared the way for you in which you should go. Look to it what tree you shake in the future. Here you will only find wind and stubble."

In former times old Mordaunt had come from the country into town. He had brought with him the strong form and good health of a man whom nature, if she does not put an inventive, sagacious head upon his shoulders, destines for servitude. But now his muscles had lost their strength. At the moment in which he was seized with shivering, when his teeth chattered, when with many "Ahs" and "Ohs" he tried to get back into his high bed, Samuel performed an act of compassion in contenting himself with a handful of crowns and in leaving the old man in peace. It was all important for him that his grandfather should live yet some time longer, and that the Vicar of Pemford should not immediately become his sole heir. A considerable time must elapse, he thought, between this present period of his betrothal with Ellinor and their marriage, and during that space of time his grandfather's health appeared to him indispensable.

"Send for the doctor and drink some Arabian tea; it has often done you good before," said Sam with an access of filial sympathy, and then he left his grandfather alone with his girdle, with the mysterious covering at the foot of his bed, with the cash-box in the old brown cup-board, with the stairs where a rope served as bannisters, with the great entrance hall below where trash of all kinds scarcely left a passage for one to pass through, with his attendant spirits who bowed and nodded with inquisitive looks as they passed through small glass doors out of the little rooms right and left, filled with al lkinds of strange articles for sale as, for instance, with immense cables or with leather goods, and left him also with the large bell at the low entrance whose double strokes served to inform his grandfather upstairs whether the door, after having been opened, had been properly shut again.

It was still raining. Sam sprang into the one-horse-coach the boot of which was made like a large lantern and almost touched the ground. He gave orders to be driven direct to Cavendish Street to the sign of the "Flying Horse."

CHAPTER V.

The Bracelet.

NOTWITHSTANDING the inclement weather Samuel Mordaunt did not find either his future father-in-law or his destined bride, the fair Ellinor, at home. With regard to the former this meant that he was not to be seen. Samuel knew this peculiarity of the old man. The servants could not say in plain terms that Mr. John was still upstairs in his bedroom and probably also still snoring among the feathers. It was one o'clock; business was at its height in the City. Inside this house, morning appeared only just to have dawned.

The servants, who had lately been changed, informed him that Ellinor was out with Miss Kitty, who was still retained about Ellinor's person. But Sam did not know this lady. The handsome dress bought six months ago had lain aside unmade until the present time, when at length Sam's coming was announced. Now it was not easy so suddenly to get it made up with all the puffs and ornaments, with which ladies in those days delighted to adorn their clothes. Her father did not wish the trouble of having the dress made in the house; he preferred that such things should be done out of it, therefore Ellinor was obliged sometimes to go twice a day to try it on. In those days a new dress was, even to wealthy people, an event in their lives.

It is true that the new servants did not know Mr. Samuel Mordaunt by sight, yet they were well aware of the important part he was to play in the history of their master's house. As soon as they heard his name, they offered their congratulations with all the quiet and respectful gravity which characterized the manners of that period. Sam had long since known how to raise himself from the sphere into which too close contact with his grandfather would have confined him. He was thoroughly conscious of his emancipation. He was so at this moment when he shook his head at his father-in-law, who lay in bed till one o'clock in the day. He possessed fashionable assurance sufficient at the same time to listen to the chattering of the new parrot and afterwards to request that he might ascend the carpeted stairs of this house, which was pervaded by a ghost-like stillness, in order that he might see the drawing-room of his betrothed. He then assembled the servants and drew a comparison between the past years of his life and his impressions of the present, and all this in one and the same moment.

Bab, the newly-fledged inhabitant of the house, seemed to feel himself quite grand in a large cage, which was fastened to a strong red cord hanging from the ceiling. The warmth from the chimney seemed to the bird like the climate of its own native home. It generally looked in a confiding manner round this room, consecrated by the innocent taste of a young girl. Some needle-work lay on a little table in one of the windows, which had not seen the sunlight for a long time. A monthly rose with its poor little red-tipped buds and pale faded flowers stood in a gaily ornamented flower-pot. On the walls were Dutch engravings in poor, narrow frames; wood-engravings of sea-fights lay in some large quarto volumes on a sofa, in which was more wood than cushions and which was covered with white lacquer and had gilt ends. They lay open as though the owner of the room or her father had just been looking at them. Defoe's "Robinson Crusoe" was not to appear till some years later as a favourite book of its time. As yet the histories of filibusters, journeys to Patagonia which owed their origin to the taste for the adventurous which at that time was making many bold discoveries, gave food and nourishment to life during that period which was in Germany one of complete stagnation.

Sam appeared not to be unconscious of the pleasure which is generally felt at the sight of such a room, when the visit is unexpected by its occupant. Although he wished to declare himself ready to wait until Ellinor's return he drew back quickly, driven away as he said by the horrid bird which screamed at him like an angry turkey-cock. He stopped his ears that he might not hear the noise, left messages for the father and daughter, said that he would return again in the evening at latest and quitted the quiet, mysterious house after pressing a bright crown into the hand of each of the servants who attended upon him. This appeared to be the inaugurative ceremony marking his future position in the house.

In his heart the young student was delighted to have finished with the attentions, which he had to pay to two men who were to be so nearly related to him. With Samuel Mordaunt the heart was a piece of ballast only put into the ship in order to be moved again to any place where it may be required. But sometimes his ungovernable passions, such as are in every human soul, and which in his were firmly rooted and inalienable, broke forth; then immediately warmth became heat, heat fire. Yet he knew perfectly how to hold the reins over his wishes and to govern himself. But when he did this it was always for some reason. Thus the controlled power of his will only gained so much the more in strength and rose up again with an elasticity, which often would have gone far beyond its object, if even in the midst of his passion this peculiarly organized being had not known how to govern himself, so as to enjoy even happiness in moderation. Not that he had always been contented with the portion of pleasure which he anticipated. The hour in which he with panting heart should throw down the cup which he had emptied to the dregs, whether it were the cup of revenge, of pleasure or of satisfied ambition, the hour in which he should push away with his heel the ladder, by which he had crept up or in which he should treat with sovereign contempt the men whom for a while he had flattered, such an hour always came at last. But the passage to it was never precipitate, but always taken with measured and well-considered steps. Even whilst working his way to some exhibition of a most overbearing and heartless triumph, people still called him a good and honourable man. Numerous of his friends and companions really deemed him such. To this disguise of amiability he owed his influence over the sons of dukes and over young lords. He

5*

had adopted a moral, quite in the spirit of Bolingbroke, who had at that time become the Queen's right hand, the promoter of her wishes to reinstate the Stuarts on the throne and to keep the Churchills and the Whig relatives of the Duke of Marlborough out of state offices. Samuel Mordaunt hated the shop-keeper spirit of England, the trading, Protestant, republican elements in his nation, fostered by the glorious precedent of Holland. And all the yearnings of his friends were for France, for the luxury of the court of Versailles in which, after the now imminent death of Louis XIV., the profligacy of the Regent Duke of Orleans would reign unbridled. Sam had already trodden this ground in the company of his friends, had spent some weeks in the enchanted gardens of modern fashion, and thus the bracelet which had been found occupied his thoughts on this day more than the visit to his future wife with her maiden heart and large, if not incalculable, fortune, which had now for some years seemed secure to him.

He had become acquainted at the house of Lord Stair, the English ambassador in Paris, with a charming daughter of Southern France, Blanche, Vicomtesse de Champfleury. He did not know whether she were unmarried, married or a widow. From her knowledge of the world as well as from her age she might probably have been the last. In Paris, Samuel Mordaunt entered into the great world. Yet even there a being like Blanche Champfleury was not to be met with every day, but had charms peculiarly her own. As for Sam, what did he know of women? His father had rented farms. There, indeed, he had become acquainted with women of great pretension, and none had been more full of these than his own mother. The rest of the ladies were the wives of country clergymen, governesses, wives of professors who, now that he saw what was outside and more dazzling in the world, appeared to him to be all mere creatures full of deficiencies, possessing but a questionable enjoyment of life, weak beings needing to be under absolute control. In Paris on the contrary and specially in this young lady of Provence, who was half an Italian, he for the first time met a self-reliant, imaginative woman who did not draw back in alarm from difficulties and who seemed to be able to make her way without the intervention of man. The Viscountess conversed on the events of the day like an initiated politician, on religious questions like one who had thought for herself. Bolingbroke, the bold innovator, with whom unfortunately freedom of thought had torn down the barriers of the moral world, entered into conversations whenever he visited Paris or she

London, with no one in preference to this sparkling woman, who was thoroughly unreserved and whom Sam Mordaunt had met again in the course of the last year at Lady Arabella Ratcliffe's house in Grosvenor Square. At that time when she had quitted London with the promise of soon returning, she had betrayed sentiments which might have encouraged a young man who was rather ugly than handsome, like our citizen friend of noble companions, to devote himself to her with every hope of success. For she said that she herself as a matron was attracted by youth; and on another occasion when she had made some confidences to Sam Mordaunt, the king of the circle of society in which the young lawyer moved, she had declared that there was no beauty worth the name but that of the mind; that nothing appeared to her more unsightly than the head of an Antinous, the personification of effeminacy; and even in the statue of Apollo she was, according to her own account, disturbed by the want of a beard; now, "Did the Gods shave?" she would ask travestying the humour of one of Molière's characters.

Samuel was twenty-five years of age. Those three years which he had passed in studying with lawyers after taking his bachelor's degree in order to learn the strange intricacies of English law, might have been held to be tripled in his acquirement of mature judgment by time and experience.

Samuel had ordered his hackney-coach to wait, and drove to his friend Lord Maxwell who had such extensive apartments allotted to his use in the house of his relative Lord Nairn, that he could well and comfortably have received several more of his college friends. Here, in Leicester Square, Sam already found his clothes which Wilkie had brought. He would have liked to have talked to him about the bracelet, and he sought for Lord Arthur in order to discover whether his grandfather's deaf old servant had said anything about it. But his friend was at this moment engaged with his aunt Lady Nairn, the hospitable mistress of the splendid palace, which at that time occupied a large space in the square every foot of which is now built over. Lord Nairn himself was travelling at the time.

Sam under the influence of pleasant associations hummed the French songs which Blanche de Champfleury knew how to sing with such grace, such charming playfulness. He thought of the words which she had said to him a year ago, last time she was in London; "You were born to be a tyrant, Sir Samuel; fortunately not to us women only, but also a tyrant to men. Nero and Caligula made a great mistake in the mode of their tyranny as depicted to us by Suetonius. No one can rule long by poison and chains. It is only to be done by kindness, by example, by good sense. You as I see, rule over young men not by the bottle or the cards, but much more by your wise conversation and good example."

'One may imagine the effect of such a mixture of grace, cleverness and frivolity on a talented and ambitious young man, who was of that age when youth generally regards woman not as she is but as the ideal of its dreams.

Blanche in London! Sam had no room for any other thought. It occupied the mind of Ellinor's betrothed while he undressed and sought among his clothes, which were already unpacked, for a toilet in which to make himself fit to wait for his lordship or even for Blanche de Champfleury. Sometimes a sadness passed over the visions of happiness which danced before his eyes. It might have been framed into the following question: How came the graceful French lady of rank to lose a bracelet in Lambeth Street or Budge Road, in a part of the City never entered by any lady of refined mind? And why (this appeared almost worse to the sharp intellect of the lawyer), why was Lambeth Street mentioned as the place where the bracelet had been lost, a street which lies at some distance from Budge Road and at all events is rather more respectable?

Young Lord Maxwell came in. He formed a complete contrast to his friend. With a gay, careless laugh he greeted Sam who, on his part, seldom laughed aloud. Lord Maxwell belonged to a Scottish family of high rank, but only as a younger son; as one of those sucking-pigs, to quote Lord Brougham, who have no fortunes and hang on to their sisters and would die of starvation if, according to Douglas Jerrold's theory, the English government did not step in to make up the deficiencies of their parents. Lord Arthur Maxwell was, however, unfortunately a Scotchman and, as such, neglected by the Government. All that this latter had done for him was to give permission for the purchase of a commission in the Guards, which had been effected for him by a rich relation. He had as yet only the promise of this purchased commission in his pocket; the money paid for it had already long ago been handed over to the War Department and had probably served to pay for the casting of new guns. Lord Arthur Maxwell was, so to speak, an honorary lieutenant in the Scotch Guards. He had in the first place to say whether he would enter them or not. He would rather have had the purchase-money which was now lost once and for ever. He preferred the arts of peace to those of war, not only boxing, riding and hunting, but also science. One of his famous name could not fail to obtain higher promotion than that merely earned at the cannon's mouth if the Jacobite movement, which Lord Maxwell favoured, should have the upper hand after the death of the Queen. Lady Nairn had had a stern conversation on the subject with her nephew. He said that this lady would have allowed him to bring half the "Association," the "Bursa," which her nephew had joined for the perfecting of his Oxford education, provided they did not belong to that party who nearly half a century before had been guilty of regicide and who, in her opinion, were after that almost ready to deny the rights of the Deity himself. Maxwell, so he himself said, had laughed heartily at this and had given the good lady better consolation than on the subject of his lieutenancy, which she prized on account of the uniform but which he himself hated for many reasons.

"If here I were compelled to be orthodox in my opinions, I should be obliged to go to an inn," said Sam Mordaunt, meantime settling himself very comfortably in the handsome room, richly adorned with gilding and glass, which was set apart for his occupation. This heresy against theology was a refrain from his stories about his brother Thomas, who seemed to have tried to maintain his rights of birth with a high hand with his grandfather. On the subject of the commission in the Scotch Guards he expressed himself thus,

"I shall never see London again without thinking of your Highland sword as good for a spit and your helmet for a saucepan."

"Good for your grandfather's old clothes' shop," muttered Maxwell, not feeling offended. "Is he ill?" he continued in a tone of sympathy; "I spoke myself to your man Wilkie. But tell me about Ellinor. How did you find her? How I wish I could be sponsor to your first-born; but· my aunt thinks that, perhaps, my arms will have been already shot off. He must be called Arthur; is it not so? Arthur is a handsomer name than I deserve to bear and I will give it to him. You will not want anything more if you only have the command of Master Will's wealth. But do you know what I think of his business? I have only seen the little man once and then found him too asthmatical for a murderer and too good-natured for a robber, who poisons the house-dog before committing a burglary. He has just the same white hair as my old friend Jonathan Knox, who taught me to read and write and always grieved when I hehaved badly, which is the reason I appear to you to be so absurdly good. I believe your future father-in-law goes down the Thames at night and catches sturgeon. One cannot get at these except by star-light; you may always see sturgeon fishers with a long stake such as he carries in his hand and a basket like that which has been seen on his back. They give the fish a thrust on the head which sends it stunned into the basket under the water. Cords and nets are necessary for this. This is the reason why he has so many accounts with your grandfather, at whose house such heaps of these things are to be found.

Samuel Mordaunt was too much interested in the consequences which might result from his appearance in fashionable circles as a visitor at Lady Nairn's to enter into any discussion whether old Robertson were not, as had always appeared to him in his younger years most probable, a merchant who had improved his means by entering into connection with smugglers. The custom-house laws at that time became continually more and more stringent. The wars which England was carrying on brought her an extraordinary amount of fame, but also involved great and increasing taxes. The desire to cheat the custom-house officers became greater and greater, and it is difficult to guard the coast of an island. There were already numerous modes of cheating the state either by open force or by stratagem.

Many noblemen on returning from Paris made over their heavy baggage containing purchases liable to duty to an agent in Calais, who looking like a gentleman with his laced hat and swinging a gold-headed cane in his soft white hand, could transact the business by means of other peoples' hands and consciences. Hanging or transportation were the continually recurring words in the severe custom-house laws. Notwithstanding the smuggling trade flourished side by side with authorized trade (even winked at by the custom-house officers) like two affectionate step-sisters who have the same father, and are only unlike each other on the mother's side.

Among the various subjects which afforded matter of conversation to these two young men, who were now joined by Earl Winton and Lord Widdrington, those on which the first pair and also the new comers preferred to linger referred exclusively to the new dogs which these young Oxonians had met among their various friends, or the peculiar characteristics of the spirit of the age at that period, or of the coffee-houses of which at that time there were already ten thousand in London, as young Lord Widdrington asserted, whilst Lord Maxwell maintained that a member of the Government had told him that there were only three thousand coffee-houses which took out licenses. The fashion of perukes and shoe-buckles was still in full force; and a new method of boxing, which was taught scientifically in Hyde Park, was very fashionable; a double feint at the left lung and the second false rib. They immediately put this novelty to the test. At last, conversation turned to the ladies whom these young men thought worthy of the greatest admiration. But on the tide of troubled waters which flowed around two pure white swans sailed at last triumphant, Blanche, who at least was fair in name, and Ellinor Robertson. The latter was promoted to this dignity specially on this account, that Maxwell insisted in asserting that adoration of the French lady could not be vindicated in the presence of one who was betrothed to another lady. Hereupon his noble friends, whose number had gone on increasing, insisted in seeing in Samuel Mordaunt a man suddenly blessed with the gifts of fortune, who would open his coffers to them, and the more so because he had already often done this, although up to the present time he had been dependent on the aid of his grandfather and on an admirable power of invention in money matters, which may be best expressed as his talent for raising loans.

"There is no truth left in the world," said Lord Arthur Maxwell as he busied himself in sending a message to Lady Nairn's major-domo to say that his guests wished for a four o'clock luncheon of dried salmon and Portuguese wine;—"neither in politics nor in love. How can one talk of the little feet of a Frenchwoman whose face is painted all over, with whom nothing is genuine but her abominable sing-song accent which a true English tongue can never attain, when one has the reversion of two rosy English lips which are at this very moment perhaps employed in holding a piece of sugar for a parrot to peck."

"The little girl in Cavendish Street!" cried several of his friends.

"Who flies to the window whenever she hears the sound of a horse's hoofs in the street," added one of the young lords, who represented his own property in parliament and shone conspicuous during the session by his absence.

"Your old schoolmaster," replied Sam drily as he raised his deep-set eyes to Maxwell, who was close to him, and without the slightest change of expression at the speech of the youthful member of parliament which betrayed how much Ellinor had suffered by the absence of her lover, and how with the rapid trot of every horse she hoped at length to see him or to hear news of him. "Your old schoolmaster would shed tears if he heard you talk thus, for what you say savours of calumny and not the least of your slanders is that with which you would paint Blanche Champfleury. In her name, field flowers, Champfleury, she has all the colours of the rainbow, but I should have said that nature has only given the most delicate pink and white to her cheeks."

The entrance of lunch and afterwards smoking from pipes with Dutch china bowls, which at that time was becoming more and more fashionable, prevented this discussion from degenerating into folly by which Lord Maxwell and his friends would have lowered themselves in the esteem of their hostess and still more in that of her formal servants.

They treated the subject of woman with great profundity. They lowered the tones of their voices; the discussion was carried on between the young men by means of mysterious hints and sometimes even more by pantomime than words. But on the subjects of dogs, of hunting, of races, of boxing, and at length of war and politics they talked louder and louder. On these last subjects Lady Nairn would make no objection to noise. She belonged to the fanatical adherents of the exiled Stuarts and she likewise would have become very indignant if she had heard the expressions which were combated most strongly by the young lords, expressions which strangely enough were spoken on this day by Samuel Mordaunt and which had sounded almost defiant.

"I should advise those whom our modern England, such as Cromwell has made it, does not please to travel whither inclination takes them. Those who do not find our land pious enough may go to Pennsylvania. Those who on the contrary find it too religious may go to—to Rome. Can anyone really believe that England has voluntarily exposed herself in vain to the charge of regicide? Absurd! ha! to arms, to your swords! I do not deny them guilty of a capital crime, but that is all done with, and what our conscience, if it only prick us, teaches us is to carry on business in general, flourishing gains and vigorous progress in every department. Our homes, our school, our church, all desire something new. The Queen must indeed take care lest the power should again come into the hands of the parliament."

Lord Timtemple blew thick clouds from his clay pipe and by holding up the bottle of port-wine to the light drew attention to the emptiness that reigned within. Maxwell rang for his aunt's butler. A fresh supply was brought. Lord Timtemple was to be indulged as a member of parliament.

But none of this prevented a vehement attack on the power of the parliament; an attack which in one point of view might also be flattering to Lord Timtemple.

"Where else is the power now?" cried the majority of the young men and one after another they quoted various of the stringent laws against the Jacobites, the proscriptions, the prices which had been set on the heads of the principal followers of the old dynasty and indeed upon that of the Pretender himself.

"No Englishman, even were he the most bigoted of Protestants, would wish to earn the hundred thousand pounds which are placed upon the head of King James the Third," cried young Lord Widdrington wishing to prove that the mass of the people thought differently from the lawyers and the parliament.

"The proof lies with Mr. Sam," replied Lord Wintoun; "If Lord Bolingbroke would give him the management of the Treasury he would change his opinions as others have already done."

"Lord Bolingbroke?" cried several others. "He is one of us."

Lord Maxwell maintained on Sam's behalf the persuasive power of gold since it had won Ellinor Robertson for the loyal pleader.

"He will be well off," said Lord Arthur laughing and beginning to speak anew of his friend's betrothal and of the hope that all Sam's friends would venture on a solemn celebration of the festive domestic event that was in contemplation.

With apparent indifference and quietly puffing clouds of smoke from his little clay pipe, Samuel even listened to a description of the furniture which would be necessary when his old grandfather Will Mordaunt from Ipswich Street, washed and properly dressed for the occasion, should enter a brilliantly lighted saloon hired perhaps for the purpose and Tom Mordaunt, Vicar of Pemford in Pemfordshire, should make an appropriate speech on the occasion, in case his tongue should still retain its powers.

All insisted that Tom the country clergyman, who claimed the rights of primogeniture little esteemed in this circle, would find his mistake in thinking himself more secure of the enjoyment of every good that earth can offer than the poor younger sons, those Pariahs of old England, those beings destined throughout life to undergo the discipline of poverty or, as might more justly be said, not to go without the necessaries of life but to obtain them by incurring debts.

In the end however, Blanche Champfleury remained the victor in the strife of opinions and discussion. The French lady was in every way worthy to become the subject of a series of debates which to a concealed listener would have given occasion for astonishment at the cautious and grave arguments used by these young men who had such small experience of life, yet who entered into such deep reflections on the peculiarities, the beauty, the amusements, the coquettishness, the sparkle and so forth of women.

The story of the bracelet, which also came on the tapis, was quickly despatched. No one offered any contradiction when Sam maintained that the laws of revealed religion, (of which at that time so many doubts and so many difficulties were discussed by the noted, thoughtful men of the day, even by the unprincipled Jacobite Lord Bolingbroke) all tended in the present case to this, that as Bob Wilkie, a servant of his grandfather's, had found the ornament thus a sign from above was given which betokened him, the speaker, worthy to be able to offer himself to the lovely lady, be she maid or widow, as her cavalier. But they all resolved to try their fortune and to present themselves on this very evening at Lady Arabella Ratcliffe's party in Grosvenor Place.

Samuel had still some important affairs to attend to concerning himself or others who had given him commissions, otherwise he would have endeavoured to anticipate all other candidates for the renewed favour of the Viscountess Champfleury within the proud halls of the Lady Arabella Ratcliffe.

It was not until a late hour in the evening that he was able to make arrangements for satisfying the longings of his heart which beat more eagerly for this meeting than for the delayed greetings to Ellinor his betrothed.

Lord Maxwell had already been to Grosvenor Square before him. He told Sam that he was expected there with all the feelings of old times; that Blanche had become much handsomer than ever; that she had learnt to express herself fluently in English and had shown almost childish joy at re-reiving news of her bracelet.

"How came she to be in the neighbourhood where it was lost?" inquired Sam. "Did you not ask her?"

His friend, in the kindly impulse of his own nature had dwelt above everything on the fact that the Viscountess had to thank a servant of the grandfather of his friend for the happiness prepared for her, and he declared that he could have lingered long on the interesting proofs which Sam had found in the incident of this recovered jewel of the existence of a divine ruler.

But this was not the first time that Sam had thought that extremely childish in his friend

Maxwell which other people deemed amiable. He fell into a great passion at this disclosure of his ignoble birth and said that he could not but be astonished that Maxwell had not asked the ladies in Grosvenor Square how much they meant to give as a reward to the man who should bring back the trinket.

"But I did ask that also," said Maxwell laughing and looking on with perfect indifference when Sam angrily threw his handsome hat ornamented with gold border and feather, which he had been on the point of putting on, to the ground; tore the gloves which he had already drawn on, from his hands and exclaimed,

"What, can that be true? I would then advise you to go and hire yourself somewhere as guide to an old blind man, to beg for him from passers-by and to hold his tin box."

"Where is the harm of it?" replied his friend. "Listen yet a little longer. When the ladies heard that the finder of this bracelet, which they have supposed lost for six months and which has not been brought back during that time, was a servant of your grandfather, Lady Arabella rang the bell and asked her servant how much the honest man who brought it back received. He replied, 'A crown.' I am convinced, said I, when the man had left the room, that that rogue did not give him more than two shillings. Lady Arabella was shocked at my suspicion. She is so good, is this amiable lady, and does not observe that we are generally most grossly deceived by those people who appear to be the most honest. I then promised to verify my words by inquiring at your grandfather's house what was the amount of the reward; and, if he should have had the good fortune to receive the half, myself to make it up to a full guinea. At these words the Viscountess exclaimed, 'Good Mr. Mordaunt! How I admire his disposition, his talent! It is true he is not handsome,' she said, 'but he has mind and I should like to see him at the head of an army or a ministery.'"

That little sentence, "He is not handsome," was a drop of wormwood in the sweet cup presented to the young barrister, the future hero of the courts of justice in London. Yet this speech soothed the anger of the young lawyer. Maxwell in his account of the conversation threw so much drollery into his repetition of the words "It is true he is not handsome," that the effect was to brighten Sam who at this moment fostered no delusions as to his personal appearance. The words immediately recalled to his mind the happiest moment he had ever spent with the Viscountess, for even whilst repeating the words,

"Fi! fi! Comme vous êtes laid, Monsieur!" she had allowed him to kiss her hand and, when he was obliged to tear himself away from her, even to press his lips to her cheeks and mouth in the ecstasy of his proposals.

After all this Maxwell, who professed himself willing to be the scholar and pupil of his friend in all that concerned knowledge and manners of the world, was obliged to give his unconditional promise to make no further inquiries on the subject of the reward given to the honest finder of the bracelet and to keep silence on the whole subject in his future visits to Lord Ratcliffe's house. After this, Samuel betook himself to Grosvenor Square and for that purpose again hired a hackney coach.

He fancied he could already see in the demeanour of the servants the evil effects of his friend's chattering. They no longer treated him (at least so it seemed to him) with the same respect which he had formerly met with in mounting these steps with their artistic iron-work and railing covered with gilded coronets and coats of arms. Indeed when they were obliged to attend to him, and merely gave the ordinary answer made in houses of people of rank, "We will inquire whether her ladyship is at home," he burst forth into new indignation against Lord Arthur Maxwell and said to himself, "who knows whether he has not also been tattling about my engagement with this little goose of a girl?"

And indeed the answer came back that their ladyships were gone out and would not return till late at night. Samuel longed to shout out to the livery servant, "You villain, you have not announced me by name. You must needs take your revenge because the two shillings you gave to my grandfather's porter have been made the subject of conversation."

However he controlled himself and it was at least some satisfaction that he had only mounted the entrance steps and that thus his necessary return was less unpleasant. He seated himself again in his hackney coach, which was waiting at the door and, irresolute where to go, gave orders, "To the bridge." Indeed he had seen lights at the windows of Lady Arabella's apartments; lights also in the rooms which were set apart for visitors. As though to collect his thoughts, he drove through half London; heard nothing of the nocturnal uproar around him; did not remember to give orders to turn to the left to the house of the "Goose of Goswell", and only bade the coach stop when he had reached the grand connecting link between the two halves of London, the north and south, namely London Bridge.

The rain had stopped. He alighted, paid the coachman, and to protect himself from the cold and the damp fog, wrapped himself closely in a cloak which he had had over his knees in the coach. He wandered dejectedly towards the Strand, first took a westward direction, then an eastward. Here the tide of life was flowing to and fro; waggons with heavy burdens were moving along till late at night; horsemen pressed upon the foot-passengers. Countless lights shone from ships lying at anchor in the Thames; the shouts of all those who by land or water were steering their way towards some point not yet attained, some tavern or warehouse, were mingled with those of people who offered their wares, as fruit, liquor or bread, for sale and with those of people carrying handbills and shouting the latest news from all parts of the world.

Not one thought did Sam, in the midst of this tumultuous sea through which he was obliged sometimes to elbow his way, bestow upon the quiet little room where at this very moment Ellinor and her father were so anxiously expecting him. He had not a thought to give to the bed of pain on which his grandfather was groaning and tossing above the chest of gold which might perhaps soon be opened for Sam's brother. He was in such a state of mind at missing the ladies and was so filled with annoyance at his suspicious doubts, that he only saw just what was nearest him and even went into the Temple gardens and stood in front of Punch, the English Punchinello, without hearing or noticing what was going on. And yet the outbursts of popular wit ought to have been welcome to him since they referred to the political condition of England which had been so decidedly defended by him on this very day though only *par dépit*. The Pope was, according to rule, on good terms with the Devil. Punch satirized both alike. When the desponding wanderer arrived in this locality from Lambeth Street, he descried among the crowd some faces which had become familiar to him in Queen's Bench, Westminster Hall and other precincts of the London Law-courts. They cast inquiring looks on this figure closely wrapped in hat and cloak and evidently not gliding about without some intention in view, for he, on his side, also looked at them with inquiring glances whenever they passed near him. "They are spies;" he thought, "bailiffs who are on the track of some thief."

London was not so full of policemen in those days as it is now; thus when parties of soldiers became visible, sometimes marching, sometimes standing still, the thought came into his mind whether these constables had not some connexion with the political horizon which was certainly becoming more and more threatening. He had picked up from the newsboys that the Queen was in a critical state. She was only fifty years of age, this royal widow, but owing to the premature death of her children and the party struggles between Whigs and Tories which surrounded her on all sides, she had lost all energy and enjoyment of life. Should she die, it might be expected that a revolution would immediately break out. The parliament was already at open war with the ministers who belonged to the Tory party with Bolingbroke at their head, and even these were at disunion among themselves.

When Sam was struck by anything which excited his curiosity, he followed on its track with all that keen sagacity which characterized him. Thus now he thought that he perceived that the men whom he had taken for disguised guardians of the public peace advanced to some of the better carriages which, on account of the crowds in the narrow streets, could only move slowly. The carriages of that period were low, their doors and windows large; it was easy to look into the interior of them.

Were they on the track of a conspirator? Were they seeking to discover some person who had escaped under the protection of people of rank? Perhaps even the Pretender himself!

When Sam, following the impulses of his jealousy and discontent, arrived near Water Lane, a carriage came round the corner on which he thought he recognized the arms of the Earl of Derwentwater, of those proud Ratcliffes who formerly played so proud a part in Scottish history. He had often seen Lady Arabella driving in this carriage. He hastened after it as quickly as possible that he might look into it. There was a possibility. But he found the carriage empty!

Now he perceived that the ladies in Ratcliffe House, Grosvenor Square must have been really gone out driving when he called upon them, or must have been on the point of doing so. But why in this locality? Why in streets which could not possibly be the nearest road to any fashionable part of the town? Why here, where Blanche, as he supposed, had lost her bracelet only a few days ago?

The young lawyer, electrified anew, elated by happier thoughts, walked through Water Lane as though he would peep into every window in this gloomy street and count every stone which formed its irregular pavement which abounded in puddles. The houses were small and narrow but unusually high; stone steps led from the house doors into the middle of the narrow street. Every third house was a tavern like the Sailor-boy, which was a resort of sailors. Could Blanche, the refined French lady of Versailles, have wandered here? Impossible. And yet this was the carriage of which the Viscountess would indubitably make use in order to come here.

Sam now recollected that dyers and laundresses lived in this part of the town on account of its proximity to the Thames. London was not yet so built up but that in this part of the town sufficiently good courts and drying-grounds were to be found for carrying on these occupations. The old houses had on the third and fourth stories galleries on which the linen, blown about by the wind, fluttered to and fro in the evening like ghostly apparitions. Here French sempstresses and Parisian clear-starchers might live. Those days presented a restoration of ruffs, stiff lace collars and worked ruffles, even among men, such as cannot be imagined in our time.

Sam was wearied with his wanderings hither and thither, which were in truth purposeless and at all events unsuccessful. In Lambeth Street, in which he had now arrived, the hated faces of the constables were no longer to be seen. The streets were too narrow for carriages to pass each other. He entered the Sailor-boy tavern; a gigantic half-length female figure carved in wood, after the style of the painted figure-head at the bows of a vessel, stood at the entrance to invite visitors to this noisy tavern.

The company here was sufficiently mixed; here were a few common sailors; a larger proportion of pilots, custom-house clerks, people employed about harbours and bridges, townsmen who expected to find better ale and porter here than at other places, even officers with wooden legs and invalids from the recent battles of Ramilies and Malplaquet. There were also even women who, however, could lay no claim to respectability.

Samuel Mordaunt might have spent about half an hour in this atmosphere which, like that of all inns, was composed of tobacco smoke, over a glass of ale to which he addressed himself with moderation, when from the corner in which he sat, leaning his head on his hands and reflecting at the moment on his engagement with Mr. Robertson's daughter and the proximate results thereof, he perceived two young men come in. They had scarcely taken three strides into the room (which was lighted by a dozen oil lamps that gave a brilliant light for those days but which yet only cast a dim light over the space) and looked around them, when they turned again and appeared to make a sign to three other men who had probably been waiting for them, and who immediately rose and followed them. These last evidently belonged to the more respectable portion of the company. The unmistakeable bearing of the eldest showed him to be an officer in disguise; spurs clanked from the high boots which he wore. More even than at the strange understanding between these five men was the lawyer surprised at the appearance of the two young men whose arrival had evidently been a signal to the other three. Sam recognized one of them without difficulty. He was Lady Arabella's only son, young James Ratcliffe, Earl of Derwentwater, of the Scotch guards in Edinburgh. Sam had seen him often at his mother's house and indeed only lately in Edinburgh but hitherto always in his uniform with the peculiar cap, plaid and bare knees of the Highlanders. On this occasion he was wearing the simple dress of a civilian. But who was his companion? Whose this fair complexion in company with the bronzed tint of the young nobleman? Whose this slight, graceful form in company with the powerful figure and broad shoulders of the youthful son of Mars?

The hat firmly pressed down over the eyes of the young man did not prevent two thoughts from crossing Sam's mind at the same moment. The first, "This is a woman in disguise," and immediately after, "This disguised woman is Blanche de Champfleury." In a moment he started to follow them; when outside the door, he was only about twenty paces behind them. He redoubled his speed as he now saw himself observed by them; he came nearer to them. James Ratcliffe, Earl of Derwentwater, turned and made as though he wished the man who was so hastily following them to pass them. But then he would have recognized their pursuer even as Sam had recognized them. He advanced again, together with the men who were in disguise; the graceful figure which Sam took for Blanche was obliged to trot to keep up with the others.

They all turned round a corner; then all five went into an alley which was almost dark and quite deserted. Sam followed on their track.

Then, plucking up his courage, he called aloud, "Captain, captain."

At this, the three men turned, drew their swords and stood to defend their two companions who rang the bell of a house sharply. They were standing before a house with small balconies on the first and second floors, with an old Gothic doorway and overhanging eaves and with tiles laid even over the walls. All within the house seemed dark and silent as death. The youthful form which Sam took for Blanche kept its face turned away and close to the door of the house, as though on the opening of the door to take advantage of the first small chink to vanish within. And this was its object.

"Captain, what are you doing here and who is your companion?" cried Sam again, not yet at all alarmed and laying his hand on his sword. "Where are you all dragging the Viscountess de Champfleury?"

At this moment Sam pressed so closely on the young man whom he took for Blanche, that, when the door flew open, the entire group which had fallen into disorder, pushed each other into the house and Samuel Mordaunt with them.

Except here and there where a neighbour, hearing the noise, opened a window and looked out into the street, all was again wrapped in the darkness and silence of night. It was a street without any outlet and was called Fish Lane Corner. In this house a French dentist, Monsieur Richard, had lately established himself.

CHAPTER VI.

Joyful Anticipations.

For three short November days and for three November evenings all the longer in proportion, had Ellinor waited in vain for the return of the companion of her youth, whom with child-like obedience she had accepted as her betrothed; three days and three evenings, after the six months of fruitless hope which had preceded them.

Sam was at last in London! he had visited the second paternal roof so nobly and generously opened to him, without having found either his betrothed or her father, and had not returned again.

Full of anxiety lest some accident should have befallen him, old Robertson hastened to Will Mordaunt whom he found considerably worse. But neither here had Sam been seen. At the very moment in which his old friend entered the room, Sam's grandfather was shivering with a severe fit of ague. He made a sign with his hand, and then in short broken words gave the address of Lord Nairn and of the young Lord Arthur Maxwell as that of his grandson. Robertson either out of kindness, or because he felt it very much a duty to his old friend, approached his bed and said,

"If it will do you any good, and if it be a question of life and death, let every thing that we lately (he meant six months ago) settled upon the boy (he meant Sam) be drawn up by Mr. Craksby (the lawyer)."

"Away with all pettyfoggers and money-lovers!" cried old Mordaunt hastily, in an angry tone and in a frightfully hollow voice, and rattling the chain which joined him and his money chest, as though they were one being, in such a manner that Robertson changed colour and drew back as though from a lunatic.

"I am dying," continued Will Mordaunt wildly. "Indignation against those robbers of Pemford has brought me to the grave; but be calm," and here he made a long and incomprehensible murmuring sound and extended his thin hand from the bed and tried to laugh, "I shall know when the hour approaches. Then I shall burn every thing. What I have promised you, that I will stand to."

A new access of shivering, occasioned by the exposure of his hand, presented a fearful contradiction to this idea of burning things, the preservation of which after Mordaunt's death might probably cause some uneasiness to old Robertson.

At the house of Lord Nairn and Arthur Maxwell, Robertson, who had quitted Ipswich Street with sighs, received at least this consolation that Sir Sam Mordaunt was in perfectly good health, although, as they there believed, overwhelmed with business so as to be hardly visible even in the house where he was staying. For they said he was very seldom to be seen in Leicester Square, stayed out till late at night, and even when at home was so engaged with letters and writings that he scarcely gave himself time for meals, and indeed the most certain place to find him was at Ratcliffe House, Grosvenor Square No. 7314.

"Where the beautiful French lady lives," said Ellinor on hearing this account from her father when she was left alone with him and not even Miss Kitty present, who had already infused the poison of suspicion into the mind of the artless child, and was thus the entire cause why Ellinor added: "who turned his head in Paris! now you will see that John Robertson's daughter will not be good enough for him."

And she said this with tears. But she was still quite a child. And she wept for this also, that in her first excitement, when at length her lover was on point of arriving, she had begun to teach her parrot to say Sam's name, and now the handsome bird with many roguish glances, and in a voice enough to destroy ones nerves, began to make a sound like Sam! Sam! which under present circumstances sounded very mocking.

But on the third day Ellinor's grief was still further increased by Miss Kitty, who, on her return from a walk, maintained that she had seen the Viscountess de Champfleury, whom she knew well by sight in Paris, riding on horseback and surrounded by a number of fine gentlemen among whom was Sir Sam. She could not find words sufficient or sufficiently glowing to describe the effect of this cortege. In all the streets through which they passed, the people had stood still to gaze at this lovely lady and at the gentlemen conspicuous in gold and silk.

The French lady was riding in the same manner as did the poor sick Queen, on a saddle of peculiar construction, such as we now call the lady's saddle. For, up to this period, ladies either sat on a horse just as men do, or else they sat quite on one side, turning their back to the other, and were obliged to guide their horse as they could, without being able to look on more than one side.

Ellinor had no ideas of romance but those of remaining true to one's first love until death. In all the stories which she had read, and they were chiefly eastern tales or tales of Mexico and Peru, the daughters of the Sultans or Incas would even beg or go barefoot if it were necessary to free the prisoner whom they loved from his bonds, and to fly with him to his native home. Stories of unhappy lovers who were unable to meet were also familiar to her. Inconstancy, that touching element of modern literature, especially the inconstancy of women, this she knew only from dark hints; just as the character of those Lovelaces who will sacrifice the heart of one woman after another were only beginning in romance to supersede the captivating charms of poetry. But as yet Ellinor only believed in the traditions which had been part of her education and breeding. She sought all the more to cherish the thought that her union with the celebrated lawyer would make her as happy as that of her father, her grandfather and the grandfather of her mother had made their wives happy, when Miss Kitty ceased her description of the assiduity with which a slight man marked with small-pox had paid his attentions to the lovely French-woman on horseback, forcibly restrained by Ellinor's father, as she had been in her from her father descriptions of the free and easy manners prevailing in France.

"I know indeed," said little father Lobster, who could sometimes make his shell very tough, "I know very well that every thing which man undertakes to win that is great and universal in its tendency, involves in its consequences some loss to himself and to his virtues. In former days men trembled before tyrants, before murderers and unjust judges. In former days they were threatened by conflagrations and by incessant and fearful wars; their ships were built like nut-shells, terrible diseases swept off thousands, whilst means of subsistence frequently failed to such a degree that whole villages and towns were famished. But in those days a man's happiness was bound up within his own family; his wife, his children were dear and precious to him, and children sought for no surer guidance through life than the counsel, the experience, the love of their parents. Then man experienced the burning, heart-felt desire to be happy at least in some respect, and to find at least some place where he could see and hear the palm-branch of peace waving over his head. The more the world improves universally, the more that tyrants are restrained by law, the more that murder, plunder and breaches of law become the exception, and that every means which can make man's life more comfortable and pleasant is on the increase and indeed attains a marvellous height, so much the more, on the other hand, does the character of man deteriorate; domestic manners are injured and the intercourse of daily life makes enemies.

This will become worse and worse, whoever lives to see it—"

"Father!" interrupted Ellinor affectionately; she never could bear that her father should allude to his death.

"Strange!" thought Miss Kitty, stealing a sidelong glance at Ellinor who had thrown herself on her father's heart and tried to calm him by her filial caresses; "strange to hear such words from a man who perhaps has a murder, and one does not know what besides, on his conscience;" for she knew already how it was that people shook their heads so much when Mr. Robertson was spoken of.

At length, on the fourth day after his arrival in London, Samuel Mordaunt appeared. He was dressed in a fashionable, richly ornamented black coat with silver buttons; his hat was ornamented with feathers, his shoes with red bows and puffs, his stockings were of silk, at that time only wove in Lyons, and not made until long afterwards in Manchester. Rings sparkled on his fingers. A long gold watch-chain hung down almost to his knee-buckles which were of the finest steel. Round his throat, which was half bare, a white lace collar fell almost as low as his watch which lay in a large bright shell case. His white teeth looked brilliant and his rosy face was on this day rendered particularly expressive by vivacity and good spirits, as he exclaimed with a laugh; "Well, here I am, my dear and much loved Ellinor. Forgive me, father John, that I have not come until to-day, since my anxiety drove me here the day before yesterday."

"The day before yesterday! it was three days ago," said father John.

"Was it really so long ago? the time has seemed to me an eternity."

"An eternity! And yet you thought it only the day before yesterday; ha! ha!" laughed the old man who had determined for his child's sake to appear perfectly satisfied.

"I must say," replied Sam, trying to make things better, "I am obliged to make good use of my time, to dispose of the hours by minutes. Thus I only knocked at one man's door in the evening when I had promised to be with him at noon. Another time I was obliged on the following day to obtain help, since even at mid-night my business was not yet ready. This always happens when one sees a house on which a lawyer's sign is hung with any prospect of success. But there, where so many live I cannot make my residence; still less could I give my little wife such dark windows as I have had in Middle Temple Lane. Oh! and I have also been detained by visiting those old Justinians in

Lamb Court and drinking with each a glass of claret to the welfare of Hugh Grotius and to my future use of a whole hundred weight of stamped paper. They all wish me success. Each has some old complicated case which he will make over to me. Yes, Ellinor, yes, Papa John, I have been looking for some pretty friendly and trustworthy bough in which to make our nest."

"And where have you found it?" broke in the old man upon this very easy and plausible speech, whilst Ellinor stood abashed, allowing her hand, which had become icy cold, to remain in that of her lover.

This practical application, which the father immediately made from a confused speech, did not seem to be very convenient to Sam. He had evidently not taken a single step towards obtaining a suitable house for his lawyer's sign. With a whistle and a laugh and a peculiar knitting of his black eye-brows, he said, "I will tell you that next time; nothing is ready yet."

He made as though the address would be too astonishing; the whole details of his settling himself too charmingly captivating and too minute to be detailed at present. At some more favourable moment all should be told, to the supreme satisfaction of every one.

In the mean time he complained of the noise of

the parrot, declared himself jealous of every thing which could win any proofs of affection from his betrothed, even of the bird, even of Miss Kitty whom he immediately tried to win over by various flatteries. He repeatedly pressed Ellinor to his heart so that his hard watch case hurt her and she endeavoured to keep at a distance from him. She believed every thing that he told her; half unconsciously she received his endearments. She did not contradict him when he asserted that at the present moment all the hopes of his life were fulfilled, that in Ellinor he should find every thing, distinction, title, splendour, yes even the most unexpected wealth. This last expression slipped from him unawares. He made a complimentary bow towards her father and tried immediately by some excuse to explain away the dubious meaning of this word.

The old man was so much under the necessity of saying to himself, "your choice was well made, your acquiescence in the request of old Will Mordaunt was judicious," that he was only too well prepared to see every thing in the light in which it was represented to him by the skilful young lawyer. He tried to make his beloved child discard her timidity. He talked jestingly of his wealth, he tried thus to increase Ellinor's shy smiles and to excite them into a hearty laugh, and said;

"But who is to marry you? The Vicar of Pemford? Ah, he will indeed for once wear a very sedate and grave face when he joins your hands together and has to wish you long life and happiness! And although your grandfather has a very bad cough and ague, so that when he shivers one may almost imagine one hears his very bones rattle, yet he will live to be as old as Methusalah. And the reverend gentleman himself will often be invited to dinner by his younger brother, so that you, or I may say we, in case you should invite your old father also, may give zest to appetite by the sight of the patience and humility which he exhibits, he, the eldest son of the house in Ipswich Street, the future Bishop of Winchester."

There was something bitter and sardonic in Sam's laugh. It seemed as though a bird of prey were hovering over a peaceful picture of meadow flowers, and innocently grazing lambs. And indeed Sam felt an emotion almost like pity as he listened to the bustle made on his account in the house, the running up and down stairs, the sounds of preparation for a meal of which he was to partake. For it was a thing quite taken for granted beforehand that he was to remain, and give up a few hours to his new relations in life; he had already arranged a method for getting away later on. Sam Mordaunt was a practiced actor. He could play a part which he had prepared and learned beforehand and make it appear like artless nature.

"Little Lobster" took charge of his own cellar. Thus on this day he himself brought up all the wine which was to be used. He also went into the kitchen, which was near the cellar. He had for some time past had a Welsh cook, and it was necessary to give her minute directions how Sam liked his meat roasted and what pudding he preferred.

But before attending to these things Robertson must draw aside the curtains of his work-room and look carefully over the papers on his writing table (which on this day seemed to be of importance) and put several of them into his pocket: above all, he wished to put a handful of gold pieces into a purse which Ellinor had made for the purpose. He also took two gold rings from a little box, but these he replaced carefully in the cotton wool in which they had been lying; however, he put the little box into his pocket. He then looked cautiously round on all sides, and fastened the door of the room. This done, he opened the cupboard in the wall, but only cast a hurried glance within it. He was moved by strange thoughts. Here among lumber, large baskets and old clothes stood a chest, the counterpart of that which old Mordaunt had under his bed. "Shall I, too, make mine fast to my girdle?" he may have thought, with a presentiment of that which Sam would one day require as a dowry. Then he sat down to make various calculations, intentionally leaving the young people alone upstairs. "They will certainly improve each other!" he murmured to himself.

The young people enjoyed their happiness. Formerly they had frequently been alone together. But never under the same circumstances as now. Ellinor now spoke boldly of the Viscountess de Champfleury, and of her graceful horsemanship, and asked whether he were the (she did not say pockmarked) gentleman whom Miss Kitty had observed in her train? How unconstrainedly did Sam laugh! How many good jokes did he not make on the vanity and folly of this lady who was only courted by himself and his friends because she was to marry the young James Ratcliffe, Earl of Derwentwater; and because on this account his mother had already taken her to her heart. He told one anecdote after another about her, which showed his interest in the splendid appearance of this lady to be but very moderate in degree and showed also that throughout it had never endangered his real taste, his true choice (and at these words he kissed both Ellinor's hands). He said that he had only ridden out with her to please his friends. And then, though affecting indifference.

he forgot himself at the sight of the little spinnet which stood in one corner of this cheerful room, opened the instrument, sat down before it and struck some of the chords (which he knew) of a song that this Circe warbled enchantingly and which even now lingered in his ear and would not be banished.

"But do you take this seat yourself," said he at length breaking through his reveries by a strong effort, "come my darling, my little turtle dove, sing to me! Play something that you have been learning. But no, play your old songs. Do you still remember the evening song of the boatmen on the lake of Killarney? That lovely air with the echo resounding so softly over the blue waters?"

He hummed the air. His voice was not trained, but it was clear and expressive. One might have thought that his whole soul was poured forth in this song, his feelings finding expression in tones rich and full as those of the harp of an ancient minstrel whose strings contained within them the very life of a whole people, the yearnings of a bye-gone age.

Ellinor did everything which this strong, determined man asked of her. She brought her flowers to him when he spoke of the delicious perfume in the room, or pointed to the little garden below in which the bright green ivy seemed to endeavour to climb up to them from the wall of the outbuildings.

When, talking of the air which was stirred by a breeze almost like that of spring, he opened the window, and then shuddering at the cold, shut it again, she sprang to the fire and threw on fresh logs of wood. And when Sam, with a glance at screaming Bab, said he felt that his nerves had become weakened by the amount of reading and writing he had been obliged to get through, she immediately covered the brass cage with a handsome Indian handkerchief.

"Now the bird will dream that it is in India again," she said, and she talked of how nature must there be so varied in its colouring, the evening so mild and glowing. She showed him books and pictures of India which she had been diligently studying.

At length she seated herself at the spinnet and played the Killarney boat-song, without however singing it. Her heart seemed to be in her throat, as she said, half laughing, half crying. She then played a festive ode from Dryden, the music of which was composed by Handel, the promising star of that day. Next a touching song from "Rinaldo," one of the new operas of the day lately composed by the same young master. At last, when she heard her father in the distance giving orders, and heard the rattling of the silver on the table, she played an air from Lord Lansdowne's "No magic like love." Her manner while seated at this, as yet, imperfect instrument was charming. Often she bent her pretty little *nez retroussé* almost down to the notes, in apparent vexation because she could not at once play some difficult passage. Then again she would turn her little head, with its ringlets and ribands, half over her shoulder, and over the white lace collar round the throat of her heavy dress of green woollen material embroidered with hundreds of tiny flowers. This was the dress which she had bought on the day of her expedition in the sedan chair. The pattern was chinese, as were all patterns at that time; especially those on plates and basins which were made of the new and costly kind of porcelain. The glances from her blue eyes and the bendings of her head towards Sam who was sitting behind her, and now came nervously forward, were rendered even more effective by a little artifice suggested by the young lady from Paris.

She had with a brush put some India ink on her eye-brows and even round her eyes. Ellinor asked her lover whether this was becoming to her and whether such additions to nature could be in accordance with the Word of God. By this means Sam found a new opportunity of winning a friend in Miss Kitty. He praised her experience, her knowledge of the world, her acquaintance with the fashions, and did not find the little pencil strokes obnoxious either to the Scriptures or to the Paris fashions.

The young people were, at length, summoned to a room on the middle floor, where Ellinor's father was waiting for them at a table loaded with massive plate. Miss Kitty undertook the waiting at table, which is comparatively easy at an English meal, at which almost all the dishes are put on at once. The last of those servants, who lived out of the house and were continually coming and going, had not yet been replaced by new ones. For Mr. Robertson was peculiar in his choice of the persons in whom he should place confidence, and if any one of his servants showed himself particularly attentive, he never willingly kept him long. But he procured for him a better situation.

The dishes were, so far as had been possible in the hurry, well selected and well cooked, and no better or purer wines could have been found in London.

"My toast shall be," said the old gentleman, before raising the last glass to his lips, "That the blessing of God may rest upon you and that the saying of the Sacred Scriptures, 'It is not good for man to be alone,' may be proved in you so that you may both experience how much better it is that you should have become man and wife. To a man his wife is a spur to lofty deeds. She increases his ambition. She diminishes it also ever afterwards. For she is a drag upon all excessive rashness. What would have become of us men if Providence had ordained that each one should be compelled to pass through life alone without any ties, without any family! Yet, without doubt, Heavenly Wisdom would even then have taken care that His wonderful creation should no less have fulfilled the object of its existence. However, His Omnipotence has arranged differently, we are to live in pairs and not for ourselves alone. Such is the fulness of Wisdom and thus have discretion, forbearance, kindness and love come into the world. May they dwell with you!"

"With us three!" interrupted Samuel, shaking the hand of the speaker with his right hand, while with his left he raised a large glass full of amber-coloured wine to his lips.

Ellinor wept; and, indeed, for joy, at the kindliness of her lover. The latter used every exertion to efface the uncomfortable impression of his three days' absence. He talked incessantly, made jokes and said all sorts of droll things. He said that he would copy out the words which their father had just spoken, and would send them to his brother, so that the latter should have no need to copy his next matrimonial exhortation from a book, but might be able to use something original. Indeed, during the progress of this sumptuous meal and in consequence of the wine of which he had partaken almost too freely, he even ventured upon the following outbreak of his merry mood, "Father John, if you should some day find yourself behind the iron gratings of Newgate—"

"What for?" interrupted Robertson, smiling, it is true, yet a little taken aback; whilst Ellinor in dismay let fall her fork which she was in the act of raising to her lips. Newgate was the prison which people generally only left to go to the gallows or for transportation.

"On account of your false guineas," replied Sam with a loud laugh, suddenly, however, forgetting his wit when Robertson, in apparent confirmation of the accusation of coining, took his purse from his pocket, held it up high and jingled the gold pieces that were in it.

"What will happen then?" replied the old man drily and quite calmly; able now to equal his perplexed companion in presence of mind. For the latter had immediately guessed for whom these guineas were intended. The purse was so new, so fresh in its colours; and when her father held it up, Ellinor had cast down her eyes abashed.

"Then," continued Sam, "by your virtue and by the wisdom of your sayings you will convert all your comrades in Newgate."

"And I hope," replied Robertson, turning the subject again to what was harmless; "and I hope I shall incline every judge to leniency."

The topic, suggested by Sam, was discontinued when Kitty entered the room. She brought in the dessert which consisted of delicate pastry and fruits, among the latter of which were even Spanish grapes which, carefully packed in saw-dust, were sent over by sea. Every here and there some little pieces of this saw-dust still stuck to the costly grapes, which were almost like small plums.

"One thing suits this person, another, that," said the old man, collecting the atoms which the others were carefully blowing from off the swelling fruit, "It suits me to sleep till eleven o'clock and to stay awake till one. If I do go out often at night, I am obliged to get up and move about. For I suffer from heart-burn, my chest must expand itself. Then I come home revived and sleep well. They are happy who pass quiet nights."

Ellinor was affected. She had never before heard her father say so much on this delicate subject, which she had been taught to consider as one which it did not become a child to inquire into. She thought that she could perceive from this how full of importance was the new position into which she was now entering. Her father now felt again in his pocket and appeared about to speak some grave words but disappointed the expectations of his son-in-law elect as to an intended present of the purse, when he said, "Yes, it is the custom for people to mark by some outward sign or symbol any negotiation which is of importance to them. When I buy a horse or a house I give earnest-money for it."

Here, according to Sam's ideas which went to the purse, the old man ought to have stopped speaking, for Miss Kitty came in the room and brought with her a gigantic specimen of English country produce which was on this day to be cut for the first time with a large silver knife which lay upon it, and this was a Cheshire cheese. Together with the solemn gift of the purse, Sam had also expected some explanation as to Ellinor's dowry and as to the amount of his father-in-law's fortune.

But the words just spoken only had reference to the engagement rings; the most solemn moment of the repast, at all events to Ellinor.

Kitty stood still as though prepared to pray.

Ellinor actually clasped her hands in prayer, and Mr. Robertson prayed from his heart.

"Lord, give Thy blessing on this betrothal," said he, lifting his eyes towards Heaven; "may the tie which binds them together serve to increase in them all wisdom and virtue, gaining for them Thine especial favour and rejoicing their guardian angels in whose persons, without doubt, they as well as your parents, my dear son, and your mother, Ellinor, are found among the heavenly hosts around the Eternal throne."

Tears choked the old man's voice; Ellinor leaned her head on the shoulder of Sam, who put his arm round her and thus managed skilfully to conceal the first extraordinary withdrawal of his hand, as though he had been ashamed to accept a well filled purse as the first earnest of his hopes.

Sam took the rings; presented Ellinor with the one which was destined for her slender hand and knew how appropriately to express his joy that both alike fitted so well; his equally with her's. He only complained that the first and welcome care which this new tie of affection brought with it, namely the purchase of the betrothal rings, had been taken out of his hands. At length he obtained the purse. But this was not until they had risen from their meal and the old man had smilingly praised his daughter's skill in all kinds of embroidery and fancy work.

"To spin your wedding linen would mean to point your hopes of a lasting union to a time when I, perhaps, shall be lying beneath the green sod. Yet I almost think that a year must elapse first. I should not like that Tom, your brother, were not married until after you. Let him and the Alderman's daughter be first! Then, my dear son, the light, merry thing that has first been first made for you will not prove delusive and it may be supposed that in four weeks all might be ready—"

Whilst he was still saying these words and as Ellinor, who perceived that something was going on, turned aside, the "merry thing" fell into Sam's coat pocket. Her father had himself put the purse inside the opening.

"By Jove! but I hardly dare touch this present," cried Sam. "Is it not wonderful to see how fine the work is! It seems almost as though I touched the guineas which, at all events, I can make use of. Ha! What jokes you play upon me!"

Sam ceased speaking. His fingers, skilled in rapid calculations of rouleaux of gold (he had gained his practice at the gaming tables of both Bath and Paris), had counted in a moment the probable amount of the earnest-money. He hastily checked his expressions of joy and surprise. The sum was a large one. Nothing could have come more acceptably to him at that moment; and what did not he promise himself in the future?

When they went upstairs again to Ellinor's room which was comfortably warmed, and walked over the soft Indian carpets and returned to the beautiful decorations on the walls by the winding staircase, a banquet was arranged at which the betrothal, which had now taken place only in the presence of their three selves, was to be confirmed and sealed before a larger circle.

In the enumeration of the people who should be invited on this festive occasion, Sam made this unaffectionate remark;

"Lucky, that my grandfather is ill! otherwise we should have been in the difficulty of being compelled to invite him."

What could he do to efface the bad impression made by these words, and to quiet the protesting "Oh! Oh!" of John Robertson, and what skilful excuses and explanations of what he had meant to say, did he not make to get himself out of the dilemma! On those occasions on which Sam perceived that some one of his observations met with no response, his presence of mind always stood out in glowing colours. For he abounded in clever expedients. He would change his tone into one of sparkling wit and humour. Generally, he allowed the obnoxious remark to pass unretracted, but overlaid it with other remarks, heaped assertion upon assertion, and at last collected such a Babel of paradoxes that he won the laugh over to his side, and compelled those who had contradicted him to acknowledge their mistake in the chief points of their accusations.

He now described the despair of old Will Mordaunt if he should be compelled to hunt up from his stores of old clothes, the best of the coats, the warmest stockings, the most respectable hat, and even a sword besides, and then be obliged to get into a coach, and to leave the care of his house, which in his absence he must intrust to some other person, to Bob Wilkie, and all for the sake of walking about these floors, trying to make conversation with the guests, and talking of the chances of peace or war and the latest prices of wool and butter; all this he depicted in such a lively manner that Ellinor could not leave off laughing. "Only think," he said, "whilst the old gentleman was here in the midst of the fine ladies and gentlemen, Bob might leave this or that door unlocked, or might lock others which ought to remain open: as for instance, the doors and windows in the clothes' room, whereas it is only open doors and windows that guarantee the thorough draught which is his only preventive for keeping the clothes from moth. I repeat, it is a kind destiny who wills not that under these alarming circumstances he should let one of your handsome white plates fall, or spoil the new silk dress of the wife of the bookkeeper at the East India House, who is so friendly to you, Sir, with the sauce for the turkey, which bird, by the way, is acknowledged to be the best in the poultry parcel not even excepting the goose. Perhaps, Ellinor, this lady's worthy husband, Mr. Pincherley, may entertain the laudable intention of giving us on the occasion of our betrothal a silver table service, three pounds weight, without the alloy. But would he do this if Will Mordaunt had ruined a dress of my Lady Pincherly's which likewise on its part is one of the necessary expenses of witnessing Ellinor Robertson's marriage! Oh, no, let us admire the wisdom of Heaven in this! The gout will not kill my grandfather. My brother has read all the books upon gout and has studied them as thoroughly as Buxtorfs' commentary on the Old Testament. The gout, as he told my grandfather when last he took leave with a secret expression of very unallowable wishes and hopes, the gout is only dangerous when it attacks the stomach or heart.

But my brave old grandfather has always known how to take good care of just these very two organs. No, no, he will live a long time yet. But it is fortunate that we can say to him; 'What a pity, grandpapa, that our feast should lack its truest lustre! Why must you choose just this time to be ill? You should have opened the day with the grand Welsh festival dance, seven times round, across and away under the arm, for which one had need have both arithmetic and mathematics in one's head. For how easily the couples go all wrong! And well as you have been able to reckon all your life long, it is still possible that you would have counted more rounds than were wanted in the round dance at the wedding, though the surplus did not concern you. What a joke that would have been! How you would have laughed!' O, indeed, he can laugh, can old Will, especially when he has a good balance! But I wager, Ellinor, that he will send us a cake, inside which he will have had a new guinea baked."

Sam knew, after this manner, not only how to be entertaining in a tête-à-tête but also how to amuse large companies: he was at home alike in the boudoir and the drawing-room. Then his eye would sparkle. Then he would stand up and skip about like a wild foal and, as it were, threatening to fling out playfully. He was then even handsome and everything of wit seemed, so to speak, to shoot towards him, as though claiming kindred with him. In this character he was known at Lady Arabella Ratcliffe's, and in it also had Blanche, the French coquette, found him again; although, as he himself said, losing many of his advantages by talking in a foreign language.

He was now beginning to sigh for Grosvenor Square, and had already made all his preparations for going thither, although he was stopped in pulling out his watch by a decided protest from both father and daughter. The former even talked of going to one of the small theatres, where at this moment a company of jugglers were playing who were very popular. But Sam made use of this very proposal to obtain his freedom. He knew that John Robertson delighted to talk of the play, "No magic like love," as a favourite piece in his young days; so he lingered a little at the talk about the theatre and then said;

"I must own, Sir, that this evening and indeed within the next hour I am to be at Lady Arabella—yet no—

"Well, what is it?" asked the father.

"Well, I expected to meet there the old Lord Lansdowne, the author of that exquisite piece, "No magic like love."

"See that! See!" said Robertson.

"He is always cheerful and gay, is the old gentleman. But—"

"Well, but what?"

"I became acquainted with his son at Oxford. He wished to present me to his father: but of what use—"

"Nay, nay, interrupted Robertson, and he described the influence of Lord Lansdowne with the ministers, the talent of the old lord, in making use of the outbursts of enmity between Lord Bolingbroke and Lord Oxford, who both pulled at the same string, the Queen's ministry, and who hated each other cordially; and in preventing them from being injurious to the common welfare of Great Britain and her colonies; and he descanted on the advantages to be drawn from the patronage of such men. But he interrupted himself in one sentence (to the great regret of Ellinor who saw Sam looking at his plumed hat) by saying:

"But is not there a price on the head of the young Lord Lansdowne! He was in Paris and was thought to be a Jacobite—"

"The Queen has received him into favour again, out of affection for his father," replied Sam. "I do not agree with his opinions. May God long preserve our gracious Queen to us! But why should

I not make my old college friend useful? To see Lord Lansdowne would be—I thought—"

"Certainly! Certainly!" interrupted John Robertson who was, however, evidently perturbed. He cast his eyes down, as though he could again hear the betwitching sounds of the fatal play which had made him so miserable years ago, and gazed on the floor in grief and melancholy.

Ellinor now herself brought Sam's hat and urged him to make haste. These kind people accompanied him to the house-door, and were only anxious that he should soon meet with a hackney coach. They little knew that the coach which was standing at the corner of the nearest street had been ordered by Sam to be there at an appointed hour. Ellinor only talked of his coming early on the morrow, and her father whispered kindly; "You will find a cover laid for you at my table every day, Sam."

Kitty lighted him to the street. After receiving a whole guinea from Sam's purse she began to account for the rather meditative air of the lover: "Ah well, Missy, all is going on splendidly here, is it not? And how good they both look! Yet, yet, if only the old man had no prickings of conscience! for what reason, do you know?"

Half an hour later, Sam Mordaunt entered Lady Arabella Ratcliffe's brilliantly lighted rooms. A great many people were there. No one thought about Lord Lansdowne. With a beating heart Sam only sought for the Viscountess de Champfleury, and at length paid his greetings to her at the selfsame moment in which, at the window of the "Flying Horse," Ellinor was standing gazing at the stars and trying to distinguish among them that particular one of which she had heard that it was the star of Love.

CHAPTER VII.

Will Mordaunt keeps his Word.

During the succeeding days all went on in a pleasant manner. Samuel came every day, and although he never staid very long, yet he came, and preferred sometimes to come twice in the day.

Preparations were now to be made for a banquet for the public announcement of the betrothal.

On such occasions, Robertson was accustomed to hire strange servants, generally a herald and swordbearer from the Mansion House where the Lord Mayor, the chief of the London citizens, lives, and has to give the entertainments necessary to his office; for this purpose he puts every servant who can be trusted to carry a plumpudding of twenty pounds weight, into livery, as well as those who follow in his mediæval procession. Or, as we ought rather to have expressed it, some of the old servants sometimes take the parts of heralds and swordbearers. These men were clumsy to a degree in waiting but were considered very honest.

The guests quizzed Sam not a little. They were respectable, wealthy men and apparently men of great worth, but their titles were not sufficiently long for one to dispute about. One of them had formerly been clerk at St. Paul's, and not only clerk; his duties, of entering all births, baptisms, marriages, and deaths in the register of the immense parish of St. Paul's might be said to place him at the head of a department—of ten clerks. This Mr. Blackfountain was a man who did business, at most, with the sexton of St. Paul's. This sexton with whom Robertson had become acquainted at the time of the death of his dear Mary, and to whom he had intrusted the care of keeping such flowers as might belong to the season always on her grave and with whom he had thus formed a sort of slight friendship, was also present. This man had obtained a degree of wealth which gave rise to the saying that he broke open the graves and robbed the dead.

"Your jewels, friend Wetherby," Robertson said to him one day, when the old sexton had himself been joking at his being accused of such a crime, over an excellent glass of strong ale, at that time called "stingo," which he was drinking in an oyster house where Robertson sometimes met some of his friends, "your jewels are the flowers which blossom on the graves! But you do not steal these; on the contrary you allow them to remain much too long and to fade neglected. We are obliged to pay you a large sum for the little gardens on the graves, and then when we come to hold communion with our friends, and to see how the daisies and geraniums look, they are all hanging their heads, withered and dried up like grass which, as the Bible says, man himself resembles: whilst your book bears an entry opposite ground 14, path 7, No 192, of the payment of a charge of ten shillings: and woe betide that grave for which the required sum has not been paid! Storm and hail may carry away the upper portion, the rain may float the tombstone from one mound to another, and your people with their spades on their shoulders pass by it quite unconcernedly, if the yearly money be not paid. And you must indeed have some thousands of these numbers, although in these days affection is rather on the decrease than the increase, and above the grave it is sunk altogether in esteem."

Besides Mr. Pincherly, who has been already mentioned, but who was not so intimate with John Robertson as to give his daughter a silver table-service as Sam had fancied, there was a member of the oyster club which met in Skinner Street, a Mr. Morton, cashier to the East India Company, with whom Robertson took care to keep up his interest. This man who had formerly learned his business with Robertson and had always been considered a good accountant, might have driven in his coach, if he had not been prudent enough to adhere firmly to the opinion, that no one has greater reason to conceal his wealth than a cashier. That which he lacked in external luxury Mr. Morton made amends for in dignity. Any one seeing him walk down Leadenhall Street with his gold-headed cane would have taken him at the very least for one of the principal directors of the Bank.

Mr. Conybeare, a clerk at Doctors' Commons and also one of Robertson's acquaintance, put less constraint upon himself. His considerable income arose from the tolls which even now every one in London, who wishes to obtain a patent, or to execute a legal deed, or make a will, must still pay at the ancient Blackfriars bridge in London. Mr. Conybeare's wife and daughters rustled along in the richest silks; and but for a certain sly, greedy expression which lurked in the eyes of this man (who, after his six years' study with a barrister was completed, had presumed to term himself a lawyer just as though he had studied at Oxford or the Temple) he might have been taken by any one for one of the Queen's household, so grand and even stately was his bearing. Yet, be it said in passing, even princes and the highest of the nobility do not generally require of their servants that they should bow at every word they speak. Hence arises the assumption, or rather the impertinence of these servants towards those who are not their masters or who have not, at least, influence with their master.

The Clerk of Doctors' Commons had rivals in his greedy, sly expression in two merchants who had formerly fallen into difficulties together with Robertson, but who had recovered their position. They were employed by the "Dispatch", to which in those days, in the infancy of Insurance, officers were appointed for the valuation of goods which had been lost or damaged at sea. Both Mr. Brompton and Mr. Tenderton were now too old for work, otherwise they would have made the advantages of their appointments still more apparent. The one scarcely ever quitted his house in the neighbourhood of the docks. The other walked with a stick and trembled very much. He was led by an Irish lad, who was made to be clean and well-dressed. But the sons of these two officials of the "Dispatch," who acted as their fathers' substitutes, were personifications of mirth and good manners. Life with them seemed to be a perpetual feasting upon dainties. Thus they had an air of cordiality and of pomposity, just as Mr. Conybeare of Doctors' Commons was obliged, in attending to wills and to marriage contracts, to assume a manner which should suggest anything rather than his silent calculation of the money that would fall to his share. Indeed when Mr. Conybeare was summoned to some mansion at the West end and proceeded to the couch of a dying person, his duty was to bear himself as the worthy representative of the fraternity in such situations, without assuming in the least the appearance of an undertaker. And even the officials of the "Dispatch" were also compelled sometimes to give up their open, cordial manners. They, were obliged at times to walk among mountains of goods damaged by the salt water, their fingers on their noses, to make estimates according to their oaths, and their consciences, of the due amount of damages and to see what might eventually be realized from these half-perished goods. On these occasions, and when they were stalking about St. Catharine's Docks as the most competent judges of everything (such as coffee, sugar, cinnamon, citrons and so forth) which could possibly come in contact with sea-water, in fact as undeniable masters in the knowledge of stores, amid large baskets full of these articles, some of which were reported completely spoiled, some only half-spoiled, (so that the Insurance money was sometimes to be expected and sometimes not) amid stores, casks of wine, smoked stores from Scandinavia, tropical fruits from South Africa or the Levant, which found a way to their nouses and made their tables the most daintily-spread in the world, what if one saw them then! They secretly sold or made presents out of their superfluity which must otherwise have become spoiled.

Old Robertson did not particularly wish for any close intimacy with the wives and daughters of these men. But on festive occasions, for the sake of old connections, they were not to be omitted. At these times they generally appeared in great state and left behind them such vales as could hardly be anticipated, and which were only approximated in amount even by Sam's noble acquaintances. Sam had requested that some of his companions at Eton, Oxford, Bath and Paris, who were not particular about mixing with mercantile and business people, should also receive invitations.

Poor Ellinor had no intimate female friends. In these large cities people are generally thrown upon their own relations. If they have none, or that those who surrounded them have died, or if by education these are excluded from intimate intercourse, then such persons must stand alone. Thus a female heart full of love, overflowing with yearnings for self-sacrifice and devotion, languishes away its days in loneliness. Certainly that might have been the hand of some frivolous person which, at the beginning of the winter, inserted the following advertisement in the newspaper; "A well-educated young lady wishes to join a circle of readers." But alas! it may as easily have been a cry for help from some truly isolated being, a cry of anguish lest she should pine away without friends, without ties. The world had avoided Ellinor chiefly out of distrust of her father. She herself had grown up with such veneration for him, who was also her tutor and instructor, that she had no clear ideas on this point and did not murmur at her fate. Early taught never to question her father about the reports which the folly of the world had circulated respecting the best of men, as she deemed him to be (for he could be very much out of humour if she asked him, "were you not at home last night?"), she resigned herself to her existence, just as it was. She was either amused at the immense size of London or it served to make her think the opposite of noise and bustle, of the roll of carriages, of the running, crying, and tumult in the streets to be most highly desirable. One can live nowhere in greater solitude than in large cities. Every Sunday, in St. Luke's Church, indeed, she saw people; and she looked at them as though she would very much like to mix among them. They assembled in numbers to hear one of the best preachers of the day; and many of them, in going out of church, greeted her, and she in her turn gave her greetings to this and that old person or to this matron and that young girl. At church they were all obliged to listen to one and the same subject, must all be silent, and could not cast around inquisitive and unkind glances. Then came a walk, or more properly, a little excursion on foot: and leaning on her father's arm they went to Vauxhall, a pleasant promenade in the suburb of Lambeth, not far from the palace of the archbishop of Canterbury, on the other side of the Thames, a refreshment for the week. In Southwark (all these suburbs now form part of London) was the bear-garden where bears and bulls were baited with dogs. She was pleased when she could draw her father away from these games (which afforded great amusement to Englishmen in older times), for she liked much better to go to the new manufactory of Venetian glass, which stood close by the bear-garden, where for a small sum people might walk about the factory and blow glasses for themselves. She had already made a large number with the breath from her own pouting lips, and had had good and pleasant sayings marked upon them, such as these: "To your good health!" "May you live long!" "Every thing with God!" "Freely given!" These Southwark glasses stood in pretty disorder on a shelf above her spinnet. For she maintained that its tones found an echo among these glasses and thus they gave richness to her playing.

Or, as may more justly be said, it was a young man who one day first made her conscious of this perception, of this presentiment of the bell-harmonicon of Verillon, which was afterwards brought to perfection by Benjamin Franklin.

This young man was Sam's kind friend, Lord Arthur Maxwell, who was brought to the house by the former, in order (though he took good care not to let the reason be known) sometimes to make up a party at cards, for which old Robertson was not always inclined and at which Ellinor was rather unskilled; or else (and this reason he was still more careful not to betray) that, in compliance with the usual customs of hospitality, he might lure two bottles of port instead of one from his father-in-law's cellar. Lord Arthur Maxwell was also of use to him in many other ways. In this, for instance, that he sometimes got quite free from the compulsory stay in Cavendish Street, and on the ground of "some ardent and uncontrollable desire of his friend to go hither or thither," went to accompany him. Coffee, although it had not at that time been long in use in Europe, had already formed a bond with tobacco. The "coffee-houses," and especially those at the West end, were the places of meeting for the "belesprits." This last catch-word for political and literary friends came into vogue at that time, as did the name of "Beaux" for eccentric dandies. The tide of those days rose high. Parties were mixed up together in a way which seemed to mingle afresh all hitherto existing shades of opinion, although as yet Swift's exclamation of that time was not realized; "Oh, that there were no other parties in the world than those of rogues and honest men!" The Liberal politicians were orthodox in religion; the Materialists, who only believed in God as revealed in the works of creation, and would not listen to anything beyond, were political Reactionists. The Parliament stood in open enmity with the half frivolous, half popish Ministry, and unprejudiced men attacked the abuses which were approved by the parliamentary committees and which introduced Walpole's notorious theory that political venality was allowable. There were noise and strife in the coffee-houses, disputings about the writings of a Tindal and a Toland once again burnt at Tyburn by the hangman; how then could Sam Mordaunt, this lawyer whose keen wit could cut a path everywhere, how could he be wanting? even without mentioning his other amusements and the demands of his heart, his imagination and his ambition. All London was in a fever of excitement. For Queen Anne whose character caused her to be beloved, and who, notwithstanding, was meditating a stroke of policy in favour of her brother, still lay hopelessly ill, although death had not come to render anything decisive.

Lord Arthur Maxwell, lieutenant designate of the Scotch guards, possessed but a very moderate fortune. He was a younger son and was compelled to rely upon the purses of his friends and relations, one of which, that of the old Duke of Argyle, had, quite against his will been the means of obtaining this commission of lieutenant which he would rather should have been sold again. Scotch by birth, he might have entered into political life, although Scotland, since her recent union with England had lost a large share of her rights; that is to say, of abuses which, however, were beneficial enough to individual families. Lord Arthur had been one of the best fellows in Oxford. He had worn the square bachelor's cap on many a festive occasion, as had Sam Mordaunt, who had declared that he would like to put it on when he should walk with Ellinor to the altar at St. Luke's. A wide gown also formed part of the dress together with long stiff bands, such as clergymen now wear. Young Maxwell was a good Protestant, but he looked upon it as a certainty that the Stuarts would again obtain the throne. It was expected that the exiled Prince James, the then

Pretender, would be politic enough, if not to change his faith to that of the preponderating mass of the population in Great Britain, yet to give security for perfect freedom in religion.

Arthur was still floating on the sea of youthful dreams, wishes, longings. He was truly a loveable young man, slight in figure, active as Achilles. It would have been a pity if Sam had drawn him down into the gulf of his own dissipations. Lord Arthur struggled against this. He seemed to feel that the fate of his life depended on his freeing himself from what had become the almost magical influence which Sam Mordaunt exercised over him. But he could not succeed. The men who wished him well and who might have aided him in carrying out this resolution, were rather hindrances, because they themselves were bewitched by Sam. His own aunt, Lady Nairn, with whom they were now both staying, congratulated him that his youth and inexperience had found such a Mentor, one superior to himself less in years than in judgment. This she had already said to him, years ago on the occasion of her visit to Oxford, where the so-called Freshman and cenobite system of student-life there—the division into definite groups for lodging eating and drinking, usually lays the foundation of friendships and animosities among the English. Lord

Arthur was in everything the exact opposite of his friend. Yet he was neither weak nor effeminate; he had a will of his own as well as Sam. But with this, he was open, kind-hearted, and sincere. His brown eyes rested with a true-hearted expression on men and things: he did not wish to sound them, only to become acquainted with them. When Sam sometimes said to him in a compassionate tone, "You are a good boy!" he would only reply quite quietly and firmly, "and you are a great fool!" And in this way he set aside the idea, intended to be conveyed in Sam's words, that he could be managed and ruled. This certainly could be done. But this management was not the result of wavering resolution, but the consequence of the friendship and respect which Sam's intellectual powers won for him in a high degree from Arthur.

Arthur Maxwell had grown up to be a slight young man, generally pale, and even with an appearance of delicate health. His hair was brown and curly. He wore it flowing down over his shoulders. When Sam continued, as hitherto, to take him everywhere "in his train" (as Maxwell himself expressed it), his young friend's health may have suffered. Maxwell followed Sam's lead, not from any similarity in their natural dispositions, but on the contrary, on account of their dissimilarity.

It was that magnetic influence which cannot be overcome, which strong masculine natures on one side exercise over the more womanly nature which it is common enough to find even among men.

That is a tender tie which binds the female heart to the friend of her lover. The loved one can even regard such a friend without jealousy. She does but see in him a beautiful perfecting of the object of her love. His friend has passed so many years with her lover, has been his trusted friend, and has also received the first true information of the secret which binds him to the beloved one. Ellinor received Arthur in a perfectly unembarrassed and childlike manner; and this to such an extent, that even her father took alarm at such thoughtlessness, and was consequently cautious not to leave the two young people alone, if Sam suddenly took a fancy to go away for this or that reason and to recommend his friend not to feel under constraint to come away, but rather to stay and read "Magellan's voyage round the world" with Ellinor, or Alexander Pope's new translation of Homer, or Milton's "Paradise Lost," or to play the airs in Handel's "Aminto." Arthur both played the harpsichord and drew very well. He had already travelled a great deal and had, together with Sam, been in France. He interested Ellinor by his easy handling of his pencil, with which he brought beautiful scenery, celebrated buildings, and curious, foreign costumes before her.

Everything in Ellinor that repelled Sam, served to attract Maxwell to her. The one found the little world which surrounded his betrothed quite uncongenial; the other was perfectly happy in it. Ellinor herself neither perceived any difference in the impression which she made upon this friend, nor was there any change in her own heart. What she possessed in Sam and what she did not, this she certainly discovered in time. But throughout, Arthur Maxwell was so noble a friend that he did nothing to call forth a change; never did a word of blame fall from his lips during the absence of his friend; whilst in his presence he certainly frequently did not spare him. A mysterious, and, to Ellinor, an overpowering consciousness of the strange position in which she was placed, only broke upon her on the evening of the public announcement of their betrothal, and by a sad and unexpected interruption.

Things had gone on as described for some six weeks, till at length a little before Christmas, the grand feast at which the betrothal was to be announced, took place. The purveying of the table had been undertaken by a noted cook in the vicinity of the

Exchange; two servants employed at all the Lord Mayor's feasts, rather stiff, it is true, but free from all French knavery, assisted the cook.

And they all assembled, with their wives, their sons and their daughters, these respectable lords of the lower rather than higher grade of the middle classes, men of worth and position in their own places and offices who only bowed the head to their immediate superiors. The clerk of St. Paul's might have been taken for the Archbishop of Canterbury himself, and the sexton, his colleague, for some celebrated doctor, retailing his impressions of his visits to his patients for the amusement of the company. The clerk of Doctors' Commons had sent to inquire whether he should appear in his dress as notary with the large wig and gown. But it was intimated to him that it would be sufficient for him to come simply as Mr. Conybeare, bringing with him his genial mood, his store of anecdote, and above all, his wife who certainly in her own person brought the size and weight of two, but who usually came less to eat than to criticize, and who noticed the arrangement of the dishes, the attendance, the plate, the patterns of the dishes and the shape of the glass, and had therefore already often been a very instructive authority to Ellinor.

The two officers of the "Dispatch" with their

families had abstained for two days from all superfluous enjoyment of the harvest of damaged stores, that they might arrive with all the better appetites in Cavendish Street, and might be able to uphold to the system of the old hired servants at the Mansion House; which consisted in this, that they joined without ceremony in the conversation of the guests whom they served, on the excellent flavour of a pike, or the compactness and rich colour of the thigh of a turkey, and even set these before the people whom they liked on account of their affable manners and liberal vales. These, at other times well-fed men, appeared on this occasion almost as abstemious as Mr. Morton, the East India Company's cashier who had long protested against invitations of this kind and who was always accustomed to make a pretext of most important preventing causes, but who at last allowed himself to be moved by entreaties to come, and (in the consciousness that he could feel the large master-key of that portion of the gigantic coffers of this grand institution which was entrusted to him, safe in his pocket) after the long grace had been said before the mock-turtle soup was served (words which the master of the house pronounced even on this occasion, in genuine High Church phrase, free on the one hand from all popish errors, and on the other from all puritanical sectarianism) gave himself up to merriment, became more and more loquacious and even grew jocose with the ladies. The connecting link between the old friends of the house and the new ones whom Sam had brought to the "Flying Horse," Lord Arthur Maxwell, Sir Mortimer Lamb, a legal member of Parliament, Captain Montgomery of the Scottish guards, a coffee-house friend as he said, was formed by Doctor Cut, a celebrated army-surgeon who was half savant, half officer, and who from having been in Bengal, was immediately on a most friendly footing with Mr. Morton of the East India Company.

By far the most important personage next to Sam and Ellinor (both of whom in full dress, in the flesh-coloured velvet embroidered with silver, which was then fashionable, sat in the middle of the long side of the table) was Sam's brother, the Reverend Thomas Mordaunt, Vicar of Pemford in Pemfordshire. He had actually married a fortnight previously on the strength of his grandfather's will, and the honeymoon was not yet over. His wife, the Alderman's daughter, who came from a great cheese country, was also present. She took pains to follow exactly the instructions which she had received from her husband before this meeting with these grand Londoners. He had enjoined upon her above all things not to forget who she was, and what she might yet become, perchance the wife of the Bishop of Winchester. Above all things, she was not to be uneasy at the sight of the gold chains and diamonds of the ladies whom she would meet, she was to assume an air of lofty indifference towards the men, and in fact, was to behave as though the History of the world had begun at Pemford and had but been continued London afterwards. The good wife only partially succeeded. Immediately on her entrance, when she was received according to the old fashion with appetizing French wines, dried salmon and slices of bread and butter, she was completely thunderstruck at the rich dresses of the ladies, married and single, rustling on all sides of her. However, as she never opened her lips at table and only gave those stereotyped smiles peculiar to provincials, and which sometimes betoken shyness and sometimes pride, her husband was satisfied; and therefore allowed himself to follow his own way which was certainly a in the highest degree provocative, and very little becoming in a minister of the Gospel.

The Reverend Mr. Mordaunt certainly thought his brother Sam very fortunate and engaged to a charming young lady, not to speak of the connexions evidenced by the presence of Lord Arthur, Sir Mortimer, and Surgeon-Major Cut. Quite unlike the "Dispatch" officers, who had prepared themselves by a fast for this gorgeous repast, which was to begin at six o'clock and for which an abundance of fish, poultry, pastry, sweets and fruits had been prepared, the Vicar on his arrival showed signs that in his visit to London on account of this festival, he had already partaken sufficiently, and had either had an excellent breakfast, or else had not long ago finished his lunch. "Your nose glows like a torch," was Sam's greeting to him on his arrival, with evident vexation.

Tom's wife, the new sister-in-law, had been spending the day with Ellinor, having wished to help her at her toilette whilst the Vicar had retired, so he said, to prepare his exhortation for the betrothal. But a mountain of oystershells at a tavern had reminded him of what he must forego at Pemford. He would not until morning visit his grandfather, who was still confined to his bed, to induce the old man (he boasted of this before his brother) to unfasten a certain chain, and open a certain chest, for the expenses of the 'return journey.'

The dignified manner in which the master of the house had said grace, gave the Reverend gentleman no opportunity to compare his benediction which he could scarcely restrain with that of old Robertson. His betrothal-address had its place at the second course, just after the roast-beef, when the question had been put; "Do you like it red? do you like it brown? (meaning such slices of the immense roast joint as were well done or under-done,) when he had already reached the state which Sam knew so well. This was the point at which, in the old rough days of academical life, he was ready to seize a bottle and throw it at the head of any one who irritated him. For to the uncontrolled passion which Sam kept down in his inmost heart and only allowed to take the form of sharp epigrams, his brother heedlessly gave full vent, notwithstanding his priest's orders.

None the less for this did Sam parody every word which his brother, who did not stand too steadily on his feet, uttered with regard to the great importance of this day. This he did in an under-tone, muttering to himself. But those who sat near him could hear all he said. Ellinor was exceedingly uncomfortable.

"My dearest Christian friends—" began Tom.

"As if any heathens would be sitting here," muttered Sam.

"Marriage is a Divine Institution—"

"That contradicts the Bible—"

"God said, 'It is not good for man to be alone—'"

"Certainly not, when he is intoxicated and wants to walk by the Thames—"

"He would give him a helpmate—"

"What did the serpent say to that?"

"A helpmate in his toil, a companion in his joys—"

"There was no toil in Paradise!"

"But who can deny that Satan made use of this companion, this helpmate, this joy, this delight, to bring Adam to his fall and to bring down upon her the curse that in sorrow—"

"Consequently, marriage must be a work of the devil—"

"He planted the tree with the forbidden fruit—"

"Who planted it, my good brother?"

"The Lord God forbade Adam to eat of this apple—"

"And—"

"The woman persuaded the man and both forfeited Paradise, and henceforth as I have said, in sorrow—"

"You see then, my dear brother," said Sam, interrupting the speaker (who seemed to intend to make a pause) quite aloud, and to the no small astonishment of his sister-in-law, though to the satisfaction of all the guests," you see that I was right when I said that Heaven really intended one eternal state of betrothal for man, eternal happiness and eternal joys, and a lifelong Paradise, without death, Mr. Wetherby, without certificates of birth, Mr. Blackfountain, without damage of goods, Mr. Brompton and Mr. Tenderton; this was what Providence intended. But then came Satan, and spoke flattering words to the woman and the woman spoke them to the man, and all was over. Betrothal, that is what God ordained; marriage—that came from the serpent! But do not take what I say unkindly, sister-in-law. Marriage has many pleasures, for all this! Now, old fellow, go on!"

It was much to be wondered how Tom preserved his presence of mind and self-control. He certainly cast some piercing glances at his brother, who had always been his superior in both intellect and knowledge, glances which ought have been all the more annihilating because, in the eyes of the guests, the speaker had on his side his sacred office and the female portion of the company, who found in the explanation of the origin of marriage given by the bridegroom little that was convincing, and indeed much that was worthy of denunciation and peculiarly strange in regard to his "expected happiness."

But Sam would not be prevented from destroying the effect of his brother's speech. This arose from the old antagonism in their characters which they loved to display. The Reverend Tom did the same thing upon occasion. From their youth they had lived unlike brothers. Ellinor cast down her eyes in embarrassment, or seized the lovely bouquet which Lord Arthur Maxwell had laid on her plate when they sat down at the table. And yet sometimes she could not help smiling at this absurd dispute. For Sam's objection which, at the last, she alone could hear sounded too foolish. When in the course of his diffuse discourse on the position and destiny of woman, Tom began to speak of the holy apostles, and mentioned the stringent rules on which St. Paul and St. Peter insisted in their decisions about women, and how the former had required among other things that a woman should never appear with her head uncovered, Sam cut short the explanation of this command which Tom was on the point of giving; by whispering to Ellinor, "We will protest against that, will we not? For to wear a hat all day and even in the kitchen will add to the housekeeping expenses!" When Tom repeated the words of Solomon; "A virtuous woman is a crown to her husband," Sam muttered; "Yes, the jewellers' and goldsmiths' bills prove that."

Yet when his brother had finished and had proposed the health of the betrothed pair, Sam stood up impetuously. He shook his brother by the hand with affected enthusiasm, and threw himself on his breast exclaiming, "Man! Priest! you have edified me, elevated me!"

To Ellinor, who was radiant in her graceful charms, and who let fall many furtive tears (though none but tears of joy) on the diamonds which adorned her neck, he behaved with such consideration, and to the rest, except perhaps Lord Arthur Maxwell, with such cordiality, that the general feeling was even solemn and remained quite undisturbed so as to give John Robertson, her father, an opportunity of adding to the discourse of the Vicar and to the proposal of healths a short speech of his own, in which he quoted the words of the apostle, "What knowest thou, O woman, whether thou shalt save thy husband? or how knowest thou, O man, whether thou shalt save thy wife?" a text which he said was the most precious, the deepest, the most full of suggestive thought of any in the Bible. For in it, he said, marriage was described as a remedial institution. Two people were united that they might mutually aid each other in attaining the true object of life, the perfection of man's sole worth, indeed that they might secure it. And the gravity of the moment was such, Sam said as though the two officers of the "Dispatch" had been coming to a conclusion respecting the peculiar laws of such conflicting assurances.

The sumptuous repast which in its course grew more and more gay and hilarious, and which was still far from its conclusion, even when, according to English custom, the table had been cleared and the brightly polished table of Indian wood was covered with wines of every kind in bottles of curious shapes, crooked, square, and crane-necked, and the men had closed together to drink whilst the ladies had gone upstairs, this repast was suddenly and unexpectedly interrupted.

An alarm of fire was heard. Certainly nothing unusual in so large a city as London. But before one could feel at ease it was necessary to know where the fire was. In civil advancement, in the conditions of social life, London was in advance of every city in the world, except perhaps Pekin. But the means of extinguishing fires were still so scanty that it was not rare for an entire quarter of the city to be in flames, and conflagrations increased to such a degree as to have attained a mournful celebrity in the annals of that city.

London was lighted even at this time. At every tenth house a light glimmered from a lantern made of thick glass in a convex form. Thus, even then, in looking out of the windows, one could discern the cheerful movement in the streets. The glow of the fire was westward and increased. The agents of a

Fire Insurance company, of which there were two in London at that time, were already running to the place where the engines stood. These Insurance offices alone kept firemen. A house not insured in them or the burning of which only endangered neighbouring uninsured houses was, according to English self-government, left to the despairing efforts of its inhabitants and to the compassion or fear of its neighbours.

When they found out that the fire was actually in Ipswich Street, the party so comfortably assembled broke up. Thomas Mordaunt, his grandfather's sole heir, seized his hat, stick and cloak, and, although he was not very well able to stand, ran staggering thither followed by his brother's mocking cries; "Tom, it is not good for man to be alone." But his own alarm and that of his wife had this peculiar effect upon the drunken man that it half sobered him. Old Robertson, who was also seized with grave uneasiness, sent one of the hired servants with him as a guide. Sam lighted a little pipe for himself and would take no part in running about on "such a cold December-night," and "in extinguishing fires."

In an hour's time the servant returned with information which threw every one into a state of dismay, that every thing at Mr. Mordaunt's was burnt. The fire was however put out; and this, through the exertions of the dying man himself. But the information was also added that Mr. Will was lying exhausted and almost dead on his damaged bed which had been almost destroyed by soot and water (the whole house was destroyed) and the scene of desolation was terrible.

As soon as they heard that the fire had destroyed all the old ledgers which Will Mordaunt had probably wished to put out of the world before his own expected death, and when after this Ellinor clung to her father and seemed to wish to prevent him from putting himself in the way of danger and wailed half aloud, "Father what is it to you?" then the company went away, dejected and alarmed, looking at one another and lamenting in doleful accents that this joyful day should have so sad an end. At the intelligence of the imminent death of his grandfather and of the burning of the ledgers, and on seeing how deadly white old Robertson had become, Sam likewise rose to follow his brother. He led his sister-in-law on his arm. Old Robertson declared that he had recovered himself and needed no assistance. Naturally, he hastened on the most quickly of all. The house was entirely empty with the exception of Ellinor and Arthur Maxwell who remained in it, for the father had said in a voice of earnest entreaty to the latter;

"My Lord, pray take care of my poor child!"

It was strange that from the moment in which the news of the fire in Ipswich Street and of the burning of the ledgers had spread and that Ellinor's wail had apparently been caused by a strange smile on her father's face, which moreover all the guests had seen to pass over the countenance of their host now almost reminding them of an insane person, it was strange that the company cast inquiring glances at each other, became silent, and descended the well-carpeted stairs to their hackney coaches and sedans (which were already in waiting) as though they had been chased down by some uncomfortable discovery.

Ten o'clock had already struck. The giant rattles of the watchmen, who glided about in their white cloaks like moving snow-men, again gave forth their signals from street to street. People learned that the fire in Ipswich Street had appeared more threatening than it had in truth proved. An immense blaze had risen up from the chimney of the house, sparks had been scattered upon the roofs and had kindled among the old rafters. It was fortunate that the night was not further advanced. There were still many people about, and the strenuous efforts of the neighbours who desired to protect themselves, and above all the herculean exertions of Bob

Wilkie had been successful in mastering the fire. The report of the messenger whom Robertson sent back ran thus, that Will Mordaunt, either in an access of fever or else feeling the hour of his death drawing near, had crept out of bed, had dragged himself into his office, and into the kitchen, wishing to burn a number of account books. This last he had succeeded in doing. But the draught in the chimney had separated the various leaves of the books already loosened by him and had whirled the burning paper on the roofs.

Arthur and Ellinor were alone. On all sides of them were the melancholy remains which a feast is wont to leave when ended. The plates had been put out of the way on the side-tables. Here stood the remnants of one dish; there, those of another. Delicate fruits lay scattered about. All order and symmetry were gone. The candles flickered, almost burnt out. The lamps were expiring. On the ground lay many things which had been trodden on and crushed; many, that had been dropped by the guests and would be sought for at home in vain. "To whom do they belong?" would be asked. Then the articles would be inspected and, tired out, every one would seek rest.

Rest could find no place in Ellinor's heart. One might almost have seen it beat beneath the bodice of her pretty flesh-coloured dress (studded with dark-red puffs and rosettes), which had become rumpled in the confusion of her alarm and the abrupt and hurried departure of the guests. But by degrees, a gentle calm stole over her. The breathings which had at first been so difficult, which had been made with such effort, became easier and more natural. Lord Arthur was working the spell which his presenee had already long exerted over Ellinor.

He had even taken her soft, white hand whilst he stood before her, and his fine, expressive, brown eyes shed their mildest beams upon her. She stood like a rose by· the side of a slender pine, such as one may see in the gardens of Italy, where the pine is a much prized rarity. Only that there, the rose, the flower of the South, grows round the Northern tree and clings lovingly to its rough bark. This certainly was not the case with Ellinor. But a sweet tremor passed over her as she listened to the words of the man who was the friend of her lover and who had already often said that he wished to be as a brother to her.

"Ellinor, this has been indeed a very oppressive day! Although Christmas is near too! How glad you must be, that all is now over!"

"Would that this last event might prove for good!" she said, and she looked anxiously out of the window into the street where now all was dark night, and where the light of a lantern only gleamed here and there.

"Do you mean that old Will is really dead?" replied Arthur, and he acknowledged a calm perceptive faculty in the vital principle, which removes those whom it should remove. This differed entirely from the disposition of the betrothed who would fain sweep away and destroy all before him.

"Then," continued he, "Sam's brother has attained his goal and you have a brother-in-law who can neither envy you, hate you, nor persecute you."

"Could a clergyman do such things?"

"Say, a man! Happiness improves many people. Happiness diminishes the temptations to envy, to malice, to hatred. Tom can then purchase for himself a better appointment which will correspond more with his ambition. This also improves people, to find themselves more in the foreground, more watched by others and to know that the eyes of many are upon them. How many even pine away simply because they live in a corner, where the light of day never shines upon them!"

Ellinor dwelt innocently on the little house at Pemford and listened to a description of life in such little towns. She was amused. For Sam had often given her such descriptions in the liveliest colours and with all the sharp touches of his wit. She was pleased that some topic of conversation should be found.

Arthur, in his description, only spoke of the pleasing features of such a town. He described a parsonage house. There, the lime trees waved before an old gabled house and breathed a most delicious perfume in the summer mornings. Doves flew hither and thither and made their nests in the old, arched, casement windows, doves with their unceasing demand for kisses. "Kissing—or eating!" he said jestingly. "Doves are very lazy birds." Then, in the courtyard, all was life and in the garden were a number of flowerbeds, far prettier than those in the gardens in front of the Londoners' houses in Southwark. In small towns, people thought more of each other much more than in large ones; everyone knew whom he had for his neighbour and by politeness and attention rendered him, as it were, thanks that he had need of him and had sent to him. And so on.

To hear this young man, who behaved so cautiously and never overstepped the proper prescribed bounds of friendship, talk so kindly, so pleasantly, always filled Ellinor's heart with secret pleasure, which was redoubled now after all the excitement she had had and amid the anxiety and waiting for the return of her father and lover.

"But perhaps you would rather sit down at your pretty musical-box"; he meant Ellinor's spinnet. "Play something of that exquisite Handel's. It will compose you."

Ellinor did so. She tried a few passages from "Aminto." When passing the fingers over the keys of this instrument a gentle rustling, tinkling sound was heard. The tones melted one into the other and were only heard with perfect distinctness in an Adagio. In an Allegro, the sounds seemed to chase each other. When the third note was struck, the first had not yet ceased to sound. In inns in small country towns, one still finds similar old instruments full of cobwebs within, and one wonders that the genius of the little Mozart ever developped itself with such an instrument and that he could travel as a little prodigy of an artist.

Suddenly Ellinor interrupted herself, took up another piece of music and said, half in jest, half in earnest;

"Handel is a foreigner! we ought to put aside all that is foreign!—Formerly you, my lord, said so, and Sam also! Now you delight in Handel. But listen instead to our sweet western songs."

She sang, as adapted to the hour of the death of her lover's grandfather, an air which Shakespeare's worthy jester, the brave Feste in "Twelfth night," sang when Duke Orsino, the music-mad melancholic, desired a song of him, an air such as the reapers sing when they come home at night, an air in which the sounds melt softly like hues in the evening sky;

> "Come away, come away, death,
> And in sad cypress let me be laid."

For a while Ellinor sang, but in a subdued tone. Then she ceased. A tear stood in her eye. This still hour, what a contrast to the talking of Sam and of his other friends! She now learned by experience that our true happiness, our true existence in this life depend on whom we associate with.

Arthur rose, indeed tore himself away, that he might not prove untrue to his friend. He felt that he loved Ellinor. He might have been tempted at this moment to embrace her. He thought he was sure that she would not have resented his embrace. On this day, she had discovered more clearly than ever that Sam could not make her happy, and she betrayed it.

"Why I love Handel now, more than I did formerly?" began this noble-hearted young man, controlling himself and trying to find some harmless topic of conversation. "Because—because the little tyrant in Hanover hates him!"

"Do not—do not—say that!" replied Ellinor, slowly collecting her thoughts, for this declaration shocked her.

Arthur Maxwell told her that the future sovereign of Great Britain, who at the present moment was wearing the Electoral ermine of Hanover, had withdrawn his favour from Handel, because the latter had composed a cantata on the peace which had, against the wishes of the stubborn Guelphs, concluded the war of the Spanish succession without having accorded to the English all the advantages which they had deserved by their brilliant successes in this war.

"Do not, my lord, I conjure you, mix yourself up in these dangerous questions!" said Ellinor anxiously. "My father says that the fame and greatness of England rest now with the house of Hanover, not with the Stuarts. But are not you too a good Protestant?"

Arthur replied with a smile. He looked at the excited young girl with astonishment. He might have felt how much she was in the right to express her disapprobation of a future for her country with which the French had to do. But he betrayed nothing of this; nor did he object when, encouraged by his at length allowing, that he also regretted the papistical views of the Stuarts, she rose and with almost passionate denunciations of that unjustly compassionated "Jezebel," Mary Stuart, whom Elizabeth had very rightly ordered to be beheaded, described the whole race of those princes who would sell England to France and Rome, as "God-forsaken." She implored him to keep Sam away from intimacy with Lady Arabella Ratcliffe and with the great people who assembled at her house, and also not himself to engage in affairs which might terminate in death or in life-long exile.

There was no time for a reply on the part of her friend, who was sunk in thought. For Sam and old Robertson were returning. They brought the news of Will Mordaunt's death. Tom, who was the heir, and his wife had decided upon remaining in the house. Robertson was unnerved in the highest degree. He spoke but little. Ellinor made every effort not to allow the melancholy thoughts which lay concealed beneath his silence to gain ground. She knew that these thoughts had reference to his own quickly advancing death. She even became angry with Sam who, with a bitterness that pierced her heart, extolling the good fortune of his brother, said, "the fellow does not deserve such favours of fortune," and declared he would make over to him all the arrangements for the funeral and the management of the affairs. It seemed to her as though she could hear her father murmuring aside to Sam;

"Well then, compose your mind! I shall soon

follow him, and that you may at least put on the semblance of grief which becomes you, the death of your grandfather shall bring a replenishment of your purse, as lately—"

Sam's transition to the subject of the burnt ledgers, on hearing these words, prevented her from taking a share in this conversation. And her father now broke off, and as Sam had thrown something almost mocking into the expression of his words, he turned away half unwillingly and gave tokens that it was now time that Sam and Lord Arthur should also go away.

Certainly Ellinor was not mistaken in the promise of a fresh replenishing of the purse she had made. For Sam took leave of her with a tenderness which was in marked contrast with his evident distraction during the whole of the day's festivities. Now words of most gallant protestations poured from his lips. He kissed Ellinor, he praised her beauty, her exquisite bearing throughout the day, said she had even fascinated the gentlemen whom he had for the first time brought to the house, and behaved in such an excited manner that Arthur's quiet "Good night, dear Ellinor!" sounded all the pleasanter for the contrast. Ellinor was obliged to allow from Sam all that the lot once thrown involved.

Sam had scarcely reached the street alone with

his friend, when he seized him by the arm and whispered;

"Arthur, I can rely on your silence. I know that you will keep what we have discovered secret and will save my honour."

"What is it?" inquired Arthur, amazed. People were passing up and down the street. The roll of carriages was still heard in the distance. Sam drew his friend to a low-built house shrouded in darkness, looked carefully round and said;"

"We are going to Wenlock Street. It is close by and opposite to this. There is a tavern there. There we will wait until we see whether any living thing is in the garden, or in the old man's out-buildings."

"Do you then still believe that idle tale? Did not the noble bearing of the old man to-day, and his words, and the loveliness of his daughter make you ashamed of it?"

Sam was so full of the project which he intended to carry out on this night that he did not perceive the tenderness, indeed the embarrassment of the tone in which his friend spoke. Besides, the darkness prevented any betrayal of the expression which Arthur's countenance had assumed.

English winters are mild. Christmas was near; and yet one was only conscious of that inclement season by the damp and almost impenetrable fog which looked of a pale yellow colour wherever a lantern cast its feeble light. Both young men wore cloaks. By drinking something hot in this tavern, Sam hoped to drive away the shivering which he had brought with him from his grandfather's deathbed, and also to stimulate his courage for the project in hand.

He dragged his friend on with him, turned down the first cross street, then turned again, and bent his steps past the wall and gabled end of the outbuilding which formed the boundary of his future father-in-law's possessions in Wenlock Street.

He said that the destruction of the ledgers by his grandfather, on feeling the approach of death, seemed to him strange in the highest degree. He had observed with what eagerness old Robertson had run into the ruined kitchen, and had there collected the shreds which the fire had left. He had also himself put some of them hurriedly into his pocket, till his brother came up and, with threats and the words that he forbade him to remain longer on his property, had almost flung him out of the house which was surrounded by watchmen, soldiers, constables, and all sorts of people. In the tavern they would look through the scorched pieces of paper which he had carried away, and remain under shelter until the landlord should request them to leave and then wait outside, if it were till morning. He thought it certain, and everything gave evidence in favour of it, that old Robertson would take no rest on this night, that he must have something to arrange in connection with Will Mordaunt's death and, not improbably, would leave his house.

This exhibited all the tracking skill of a sceptic born to be a lawyer or rather a policeman, when passing over ground which does not yield under him, but permits a strong tread, bold treatment. In such cases by seizing on the right moment his powers of combination often win wonderful success.

Arthur was angry and made some opposition: but Sam dragged him on with him and both entered the tavern.

It was a gloomy house where ale was sold and where hot water and sugar were provided, in addition to gin and rum. A copper kettle stood on the fire which was burning brightly in the open chimney. The landlord seemed to indulge off and on in a nap: the landlady, a plump beauty of the Dutch rather than English type, was obliged regularly to give him a poke when anything more than usual was required, as for instance, when change was wanted for a sovereign. She was much younger than he was, but for all that, she had not yet acquired full sway over the cash-box. The tavern was named in humorous remembrance of the times of "merry England," "The Pitcher without a Handle." Its motto ought to have been "Here one may hold the tankard with both hands and span it as a tender lover measures the waist of his fair one."

All went on merrily here. They sang, drank and smoked Dutch pipes. Here the elements of life on the Thames were wanting. Here were Clerks, petty officials, citizens from that quarter of the town, old customers who played at cards and who especially liked the "Pitcher without a Handle" on this account, that Mr. Oadkins the landlord regularly received a poke in the ribs from Mistress Susanna his wife when fiddlers, singers and conjurers came into this venerable establishment for beer and spirits and wished to show off their skill. Then Mr. Oadkins would spring up and chase away the importuners of his guests, whose business here was to give their pence to him and not to others.

Debates on peace and war were carried on here, and the parliamentary standard was held as high in this club-house as the genius of Great Britain could soar. Scotch and Irish were obliged here to submit to the shopkeepers and tradespeople of London, or death and murder threatened all. A whistle and

Mr. Oadkins had two sturdy drawers at hand. But for the most part, he slept and did not even hear the sweet flatteries which Mistress Susanna received when she gave the change of small money in coin even-smaller. These were better days than those which formerly existed in Eastcheap at the house of Mrs. Quickly, but they were still not far removed from the times of Cromwell and of the scaffold at Whitehall on which a king suffered who betrayed his people.

For the two new guests who were so well dressed, fresh water was poured from the hot kettle to temper the glow of the taffia, at that time called West Indian, a beverage obtained from rice and sugar. They seated themselves in a corner, ordered a light for which a special charge was made and spread out before them the little shreds of paper which still smelt of the fire.

Arthur laughed at Sam's indignation that the scraps were not larger. But what did they contain? Figures, here and there a date already as far back as the year 1698, the names of some articles which bore no connection with each other and which could only be guessed at. That a shilling should stand opposite an amethyst ring appeared to them quite absurd, for this could not possibly be its value, not indeed even its value in pawn. This portion of the sharp-sighted Sam's reconnoitring remained without any result.

One hour after midnight struck. The streets had become still as death. The four loud, sonorous, quarter-strokes of St. Paul's clock, the brazen stroke of one could be heard even here. A cannon shot sounded from the ramparts of the Tower giving evidence of the careful watch kept by its commandant even at midnight. Still the landlord gave no signs of intending to shut up his house. But most of the guests rose. Sam and Arthur also prepared to leave the tavern.

All was still and dark outside. One could not have recognized any person even at the distance of three paces.

"Let us go home; you need rest as much as I do," said Lord Arthur Maxwell wrapping himself with a shiver in his cloak.

"Then this night would be lost. Who knows when our parole will leave us free again?" answered Sam, but without lowering his voice.

"You talk loudly of things which are not intended for the street," replied Lord Arthur, looking round and glancing inquiringly to see whether this mention of a parole, which might possibly give rise to serious consequences, could be heard by any one.

Meanwhile Robertson's house lay wrapped in the

repose of night. Nowhere was a sign visible of any of its inhabitants being awake. They were obliged to return down a portion of Wenlock Street in order to obtain a sight over the high garden wall of the principal building in Cavendish Street.

"I should be ashamed," burst forth Lord Arthur Maxwell, "to give place for a moment to such a suspicion as foolish people entertain respecting him, and to-day especially when you have received from this kind-hearted man the most speaking proofs of his goodness."

Sam instead of making any answer, sat down on a kerb-stone, drew his cloak closer over his chest and crouched down, lurking like a foot-pad.

"We shall have some affair with the watchmen," said Lord Arthur stamping his foot.

"If anyone asks what we are doing here, you have only to say that I am tipsy."

Arthur made as though he would go away. Certainly it was only in appearance, for he could not possibly leave Sam here alone. Their road was one and the same, their place of residence the same. He very soon turned back.

Whilst Sam, cunning as a beast of prey watching at night for booty, fixed his eyes on the wall and kept in sight the little door which led from the out-buildings of the house, Arthur walked up and down and thought of all that had happened during the day and pictured to himself the comfortable apartment of the young gir lwho, with so many just claims to a future full of happiness, was without doubt on her way to a future of sorrow. He knew Sam's fickleness, his uncontrolled nature, the instability of his disposition. The crafty French adventuress was not the only person who seemed to him to come between Sam and Ellinor. Of her, he knew that she was an emissary of the royal Pretender and of Louis XIV, who was at that time still living and who assisted the Pretender. But he did not know the full extent of the power which this wily woman exercised over Sam, whom she looked upon as the ruling spirit of a circle of the youthful members of the aristocracy.

An hour might have passed; Arthur had repeatedly urged that they should go away and return home, when Sam suddenly gave up the obstinate opposition which he had made by his silence and by remaining immoveable in the same sitting position and simulating drunkenness whenever anyone passed, by exclaiming in a subdued tone,

"Do you see that? The flickering light! In the side building."

Arthur could not deny that he had seen a gleam of light. But even whilst Sam was giving utterance to his eager, broken words, the gleam had again disappeared.

"He is preparing to go out; be on the watch; we shall find out something."

And in truth, scarcely ten minutes had passed before a creaking sound was heard from the house with the sign of the Flying Horse.

Sam had risen and glided nearer. Lord Arthur followed against his will. Their eyes had begun to be accustomed to the fog; the yellow mist also appeared to be lifting; and the repose of night had diminished the smoke which rose from the chimneys and served to thicken the atmosphere. Pressing against the wall Sam crept along like a cat close to the garden.

It seemed as though envy, or the sudden good fortune of his brother induced him to wish to gain more from his future father-in-law than merely the occasional gifts suggested by his kindly moods. If he should be able to catch the old man in something that was not legal, then he would be in his power and Sam could do what he liked with him. The two friends were still standing close by the damp wall, like hunters on the watch, when they heard the creak of a door, and some one actually emerged from the building. They could hear the gentle opening and shutting of a lock and the rattling of several keys; and it was a large, dark basket which first became visible to them through the fog, together with a gleam of light which seemed to come from a lantern. When the apparition turned, they saw a man apparently of Robertson's size, but no head was visible and they could only hear the sound of a stick. The figure now began to move. But even if the distance and the fog had permitted them to see it more distinctly, they would still have been unable to recognize the figure, for it was partly concealed by the large basket on its back, and besides its head was covered by a thick cap which was drawn down over the ears. Felt boots covered its feet and rendered the man's steps almost inaudible. The material in which the whole figure was enveloped seemed to be grey, wadded sackcloth, not unlike that which is described to us as worn by the Greenlanders; his stick must have had an iron point. They could hear this by the noise it made on the pavement. His lantern gleamed faintly.

"It is he; now we will follow him and see what he is about," whispered Sam, as he glided along by the wall, whilst the figure had already locked the door, and was moving down the street with his basket, with his stick clanking on the pavement, and with his little lamp.

As the form hastened on rather quickly, and in

spite of the gleaming light, seemed likely soon to disappear in the fog, Sam wanted to hurry on and made bounds like an animal on the spring.

But suddenly he found himself checked. Arthur stood in front of him with his sword drawn, held Sam fast with his powerful left arm, and exclaimed, in a voice which seemed to echo through the death-like stillness of the street,

"Stand!"

"Are you mad?" said Sam, springing back and then trying again to spring forward.

"I will run you through the body if you go a step further."

Arthur spoke these words almost inaudibly, but they were distinct enough for Sam's ear. They seemed scarcely able to cross Arthur's lips through his closed teeth, for indignation.

"You are mad," groaned Sam, choking with rage and trying to free his right arm, that he also might be able to draw his sword; "Unhand me."

Arthur flung Sam against the wall, then seized his sword by the hilt and pointed it at his adversary's throat like a dagger. Sam laughed audibly. Distinguishing footsteps, which apparently were those of a watchman, he gasped out "You are a fool; of course it is too late now; he has escaped."

Arthur's opposition relaxed and he looked down

the street. Nothing more was to be seen or heard of the nightly wanderer.

When, in reality, one of the white guardians of the night came up with his rattle at his girdle, and asked them what they were doing here so late, they looked like two good friends who had been quarrelling, and had become reconciled, and passed on with the usual jokes to which London watchmen are, to the present day, accustomed from the public in its intercourse with their imperial highnesses, "the royalty of midnight." But how much might not Sam have injured his future father-in-law in making this watchman accessory to his observations and thus himself contributing to increase the strange reports about John Robertson!

CHAPTER VIII.

The French Enchantress.

CHRISTMAS had passed. On St. Valentine's Day, which followed soon afterwards, was the last memorial celebrated of that old merry England which was daily becoming more forgotten by the spread of Puritanism. That other sacred feast of Easter was already drawing near. In Robertson's house many puddings, only made according to old tradition and many dishes, only distributed according to ancient custom on certain days, were consumed; and Miss Kitty had obtained an ever increasing field for her influence, as it certainly could not be denied that she had seen the world, had visited various cities and knew many things which it is true exist also in England, but which one only understands rightly how to appreciate when one has met with them abroad. For this reason, the young lady was almost perfect in her discharge of the usual ceremonies at the Flying Horse.

When once the word "betrothal" has been spoken in a house, preparations for the marriage almost go on of themselves. Not that the tribe of messengers and furnishers of trousseaux do not immediately announce themselves, the companies for wedding-outfits in Oxford Street; together with the multitude of those who make a spectacle of a wedding, troops of knaves old and young, of young and old Megæras, of those battered pots, fifes and kettledrums which even in the present day are bought in London for hard cash, for indeed life is composed much more of ancient customs than of things expressed by us as according with our own pleasure. Fate is a skilful accountant; in addition, no one is like him; here, one condition is given, there, another, and the two unite of themselves. In their results, they indeed surprise us foolish men who are often not able to understand what with them is a matter of course. Why do you not with a resolute hand seize the spoke of the rolling wheel and arrest its course by the expression of a powerful will? Not one man in ten can do this, and he will not willingly bruise his hand. Hence, many a marriage dowry is granted, the day draws near, all is arranged and prepared, and the tears may fall on cambric of dazzling whiteness, and shed yellow iron-mould on the silver spoons and forks before they are used yet it cannot be disarranged because of this tearful dew.

But the myrtle wreath is not yet here! Thus

did Eleanor frequently console herself when her lover asserted that he was obliged to go away for a fortnight on account of preparation for his practice, and yet proofs enough might have been found that in London, which was even at that time an enormous place, a man could affirm that he had gone to Glasgow or Edinburgh, whilst all the time he might be seen disporting himself on Blackfriars Bridge or in the Temple gardens. Had Sam been thus discovered by anyone who knew Mr. Robertson, he would have been only just that moment returned from his excursion. Sometimes, so he asserted, he had to work all day and all night.

John Robertson proved himself extraordinarily obliging towards Thomas Mordaunt and in settling his grandfather's affairs. This last was a considerable undertaking as it rendered law proceedings necessary which were wearisome, sales, auctions, sealings and unsealings, days at Doctors' Commons, where Mr. Conybeare was, on each occasion, highly delighted when his old friend Robertson in spite of the troubles of these days, appeared before the keepers of the seal in a dress of the newest fashion, which he had had made on purpose, and acted as witness for the rights of the young clergyman.

"Why have you never had yourself elected for Parliament?" said Mr. Conybeare as he watched the grave, dignified, yet benign appearance of his old friend when the latter gave his evidence.

Robertson naturally wore black on the occasion, as was becoming in case of a death; a short coat with silver buttons and trimmings, which according to the customs of the time drew attention to the proportions of the figure, short, narrow, close-fitting breeches on his thin legs, stockings and buckled shoes which were also further ornamented with ribbon. The waistcoat had at that time the peculiar advantage of being long enough to keep the body warm. A wig of artistic hair, which fell in becoming locks over the shoulders, had already become indispensable. The lace on the ruffles at the old gentleman's breast and sleeves was of real Brussels and in themselves represented no inconsiderable sum. A round hat, ornamented with a plume, and a dress sword were not wanting. Lord Arthur Maxwell could not be ashamed to be seen anywhere with this well-dressed, gentleman-like Mr. Robertson.

For he accompanied Robertson to Doctors' Commons. He did this for Ellinor's sake. He was thus enabled to take care of her aged father and to amuse him if he were kept waiting rather long in the ante-room of the court, and even to lay his embargo on him in case he should be invited by the fortunate heir, the Vicar of Pemford, to go with him to a wine tavern. Ellinor knew that large and very gloomy pictures hung in all the old public halls in London, pictures either of kings who had themselves been beheaded, or of people who had had others beheaded, and this even from the Assyrian times. Thus "little Lobster" who had long since given up his red coat, might be overcome by sad thoughts, and come home to dinner out of sorts, and curse the progress of the world which, since his autobiographical communications to his dear child, he always connected with his misfortune at Drury Lane, and with the stories of tyranny represented there (alas! too true and not Assyrian only) with the Sultan Bajazet who was confined in prison, and similar beautiful and touching theatrical representations which, however, remained prohibited to Ellinor. Since Will Mordaunt's death, John Robertson had become sensible of the hurry in Ellinor's betrothal. Sam sometimes treated him with a haughty stiffness which could only be excused by this, that his conscience was not at ease about his relations to Ellinor.

Once also, and this shortly after the evening of the betrothal, Sam had to learn that Mr. Robertson could become angry and that in those moments when he grew as white as the wall, he could take decided and resolute steps which left much cause for repentance.

For instance, Sam once allowed himself to say: "My dear father, I did not know that your wealth was owing to a paper mill and that you went out at night to collect rags in the streets, but of late I have myself noticed this!"

But at this moment the white pallor appeared, the old man seized the again empty purse (which Sam while speaking had been brandishing like a memento mori just before him, as though it were his business to make haste and fill it) flung it in Sam's face and muttered an almost inaudible word which sounded like, "Rascal!" The parrot immediately began to scream, and fortunately its cries overpowered all else. However, Sam threatened that next time he would wring the brute's neck.

At first, Robertson saw Lord Arthur's almost daily visits with some surprise. Gradually they brought melancholy thoughts to his mind. The English aristocracy has many advantages over ours. It is rational enough only to count pureness of descent on the father's side. It has secured the imposing stamp of a grand race of fine men by this, that its members do not always marry and intermarry among aristocratic families, as the oldest authentic aristocrats in the world, the Jews, unfortunately do, as also the patrician classes in large cities, whereby a puny degenerate race comes into existence, children with prematurely old faces, "old heads upon young shoulders." No, the English gentry seek the mothers of their children from all classes indifferently, and thus always renew their ancient blood with fresh healthy elements, intermarrying even with the pretty daughters of country farmers. A marriage between Lord Arthur and Ellinor would hardly have met with opposition from the family of the former. For many deaths must have occurred before Lord Arthur could possess more than his lieutenant's commission which he often grumbled at, but could not sell without offending the relatives of the Duke of Argyll who had thought to provide for him by this expensive present.

Father John read Ellinor's heart, and he often looked with emotion at the tear-stained cheeks of his child. Each understood the other, although not a word was uttered on the subject of their pain. And once, when Miss Kitty broke the ice and condoled with the lover, not leaving his friend unblamed, the old man checked her into silence with a Chut! Chut! uttered in a jesting tone, but meant in very grave earnest.

Between Arthur and Sam, who were still living under the same roof and were indeed both guests of Lord Nairn, the old good understanding seemed to have been restored. Lord Arthur made amends by his kindness for having drawn his sword and pointed it at his old friend's throat, so that if he had advanced a step it would inevitably have cost him his life, and acknowledged his hastiness the more readily because Sam appeared anxious to resume the friendship which had been thus interrupted. The refusal on the part of the old man to refill his purse had alarmed him. He even admitted to his friend that the shrouded figure of that night might have been some other person, standing in some intimate connection with the old man who could not possibly himself be a hypocrite. The times were so troubled, parties adopted so many and such strange means for concealing their real intentions, that one could not tell what might not be going on at night in the "Flying Horse."

From that evening in which Sam Mordaunt had been forcibly driven in at the dark, open door of the house in Fish-Lane Corner, his position as regarded parties had become a dangerous one. The opposition which he had once raised in friendly circles against the claims of the Pretender was now the opposition of the controversial spirit of an irritable man who loved to do his utmost to maintain his ground. At all events it was dissimulation. He had already when in Paris joined in the Jacobite plots. On that night in which chance had led him within the circle of the conspirators his lot was cast. The Viscountess de Champfleury, the emissary and, as many people said, the innamorata of the Pretender, who flattered her with the idea of perhaps sharing in some degree the splendour of his throne, herself became answerable on that occasion for the bold intruder whom the others were not disinclined to thrust out. The dentist, Richard, lent the inoffensive, unsuspected, little asylum in which the conspirators assembled, as they had done six weeks before when the Viscountess had also paid a short visit to London of which Sam knew nothing. They had now been obliged to seek another place of meeting. For the watchmen under the control of the Lord Mayor were already on the track of the Jacobites.

The Queen was near her end. The conspiracy was becoming more and more ripe for an outbreak. The councillors nearest to the throne were in the plot. A political stratagem, a blowing up of the Parliament was to be their special aim. To bring this about, to obtain influence over the local authorities and the magistrates all this could only be effected by the participation of the army. This was doubtful in the highest degree. Brilliant deeds were coupled with the name of the Duke of Marlborough whom the present party, the Tories, who were at the head of affairs had removed and indeed banished. When the Queen's eyes should be closed for ever, then all would be at stake. Either Bolingbroke would gain the day, by the instantaneous seizure of the Elector George Louis, who was expected from Hanover and who certainly had nothing but his Protestant faith to recommend him, or Bolingbroke would be obliged to retire from the field with his adherents, and to seek for safety, perhaps even for the preservation of his head, in immediate flight. Lady Ratcliffe's* circle was watched by those authorities in London who had the control of the police, as well as by the special spies of Parliament. This amiable lady gave brilliant parties for the purpose of misleading public opinion as regarded her behaviour and her friends. Lord Lansdowne, the poet and composer, had no Whig tendencies. But he was an aristocrat of the purest water and his son, who had formerly been an officer, made no secret of his opinions. The father's talents, his learning, his artistic tastes, afforded a cloak for the real object of the assemblies in Grosvenor Square, which (although with due caution as regarded the servants who were for the most part bribed by the police) became more and more frequent at the houses of

---

* Ancestress of that octogenarian matron, the Countess of Derwentwater who leads so adventurous a life in London, in the effort to recover the fortune confiscated from her family at that period.

Lady Nairn and Lady Ratcliffe. On these occasions many of the company retired into, apparently, little card-rooms: others vanished into half-lit boudoirs, into niches which were filled with tropical plants and thus transformed into grottoes, when their ostensible object was to pay court to the beauties of the evening. But in truth, the events of the day, the aims and intentions of their party were the subjects of discussion.

It was at one of these assemblies, towards twelve o'clock at night, and in the house of Lady Arabella Ratcliffe, that two persons were engaged in an earnest conversation in a shell-grotto, which opened from a brilliantly lighted drawing-room, thus protected from the curiosity of the company, who were listening to the singing of an Italian.

The words which might have been overheard, were most impassioned.

But even a quick ear would have heard only enough to understand that they were French. A gentleman and lady were the speakers. The latter deadened the sound of her voice by means of a fan, which she held in her gloved hand. The other by means of a portfolio, which he likewise held before his mouth, when his words grew too excited.

"These are not the things, which can be of service to us!" said the lady flushing. "Writing!

Speaking! These are fitted for things, which you throw among the crowd, fugitive pieces, lampoons on our opponents! No. Deeds must be dared. Arms must speak now, pens no longer."

"The time will come," was the reply. The fiery eyes of the man glanced for a moment towards the saloon, then became once more fixed with intense admiration on the swelling chest of the speaker, which was covered only with transparent gauze, and the indignant heavings of which she sought to conceal with her fan.

"That is what you always say, sir!" she continued. "And when the time comes, nothing is ready, none of those preparations made, which alone can secure our object. But no wonder," said she turning away and pouting coquettishly, "for you are not yet free of the first enchantments of love! Oh, these fetters of your charming Ariadne which you (faithless to desert her!) should never have taken upon you!"

"My Ariadne is here!" replied he who was thus mockingly taunted, with tempestuous ardour. "You alone bear in your hand the thread which will guide me through the labyrinth of life. Faithless! Oh, what vows do I acknowledge other than those which I have sworn to you!"

"You are afraid to destroy the peace of a little

family! The tears in the eyes of your beloved are to you transformed into nothing but ballot-balls for the courts, for parliament! you fancy that by means of votes and a majority of voices, you can bring about an affair, which ought to be conducted and arranged both secretly and courageously like that of St. Bartholomew's night. Lady Nithsdale then has written to you?"

"About the garrison at Aberdeen? Certainly! But it is only that which she has heard from her relations."

"So much the more imperative is the necessity of taking every point into consideration."

"Nevertheless, I believe the information is to be depended on."

"Do you rely on the calculation of the active forces who await our orders in the Highlands?"

"I carry everything here in my heart," said Sam, and he pressed to his breast the portfolio, which he made use of to dull the sound of his voice and sometimes also to conceal his wildly admiring glances.

"But, ha! ha!" laughed the Frenchwoman sarcastically, "all still remains on paper, as also your grand plan, the winning of the chieftains of the

North, which I gave back to you together with the encouraging notes made by the Earl of Carnwath."

"This information also I carry about with me carefully guarded! I employ every free moment in completing my inquiries. See!" He unfastened a pocket-book which, in accordance with the taste of those times, was punctiliously locked, and took out a folded paper which he opened. "See here, the sketch of a map of Great Britain, which will prove of the greatest service to the Pretender. I have marked with green all the districts which are favourable to him. In parts, which are marked yellow, an energetic and even armed rising is to be expected! In those marked red, the officers may be decidedly counted upon, if not the garrisons."

Blanche de Champfleury examined the map like a general to whom a bribed spy hands over the plan of an enemy's fortress, half doubtfully, half in agreeable surprise. Her dark, flashing eyes were rather short-sighted. The holding-up of the map close to them gave a gravity to her bearing, which was almost injurious to the impression of feminine grace. But she was mistress of herself, as she knew, even when a frown passed over her white forehead. In a moment every line became smoothed down again below the tocque of hair, which was bestrewn with silver powder and surmounted by two tall ostrich feathers. Lord Arthur, who staid in the music-hall, had called this elaborately piled coiffure, a "frisure à la sleigh-horse." Her arms were bare and adorned with bracelets, indeed one was the identical bracelet which had been lost six months before, and had only lately been found in so strange a manner. Sam was so bewitched by them that he imprinted a kiss on one, as the wide, open, green silk sleeve, embroidered with golden lilies, fell back when she held his map up to her eyes. She turned her star-like eyes upon him in pretended surprise which, however, perhaps had in it something of reality, But she was only playing with him and had perhaps forgotten what she had before allowed him. Her thoughts were, indeed, set upon something much higher. She now drew away her rosy lips with a quick, perverse air, which was particularly becoming to her. Her every movement seemed to have been studied before the mirror. The Viscountess was taller and slighter in figure than French women are wont to be.

"He must land there!" said she, pointing to a spot on the map, and taking the glove from off her fair fingers for this purpose. "You have the greatest number of red and yellow marks there! They are quite thickly studded! If, indeed, you are not mistaken! Our information regarding these districts is not so favourable."

"If you mean to fly to meet the Prince," replied Sam, with all the sulkiness of jealousy, as he folded up the map and put it by in his portfolio, round which he fastened the straps, "if you fly to meet him, every bay on the Scottish coast will represent you as Dido and him as Æneas. Would that I could comprehend what has inspired you with this enthusiasm for the Pretender! In Versailles, the report was that you did everything for the service of your church, for the Roman Nuncio, the Almoner of the king; that Rome had bribed you; had bribed you with the treasures of its favour, with the nimbus of canonization for your lovely, faithless lips; it was said that you were obliged to venture all, everything, so that you might but overthrow England's church and, at least, give her a prince who attended Mass. But now—here, I know something quite different."

"What do you know?" said she, laughing.

This lovely woman might, indeed, at this very moment have been comparing the personal appearance of James III., which had in it so little that was prepossessing, with that of this man who, it was true, was also far from handsome, but who fixed his eager eyes upon her, seized both her hands, tore her gloves completely off and covered them with kisses, quite contradictory of the bitter reproaches poured forth by his jealousy. Sam's eyes flashed, his features appeared to become enlarged in a proportion which gave them beauty, his blood seemed to himself to have collected in the veins of his throat. He was a man, a hero, who in his passion of admiration might have thrown himself at her feet, had there not been a fear of witnesses. This woman's rash intrigues, her courting had been thrown away on an indolent, unenergetic personage, as must have come vividly before her eyes at this moment. She was silent. She feared to betray that in truth, she had lacked that motive for her exertions which Sam in the vehement outburst of his passion, as he now perceived, had represented as absent whilst accusing her of being enamoured of the Pretender.

"You have marked the country round Peterhead," said she, evasively, "as exceedingly well-affected. How comes this? The people there are more than Protestant, they have the Quaker spirit. How can you believe that so cheering a reception will be accorded to us there?"

"It is owing to the hatred of the Scotch to their union with England! The slight put upon them in state affairs. Scotland has but seventeen votes in parliament, whilst England, the imperious conqueror, counts votes by the hundred. The prospect of assistance from Ireland is founded on religion, that of assistance from Scotland on wounded honour, a slight offered to a great historical past! English haughtiness wounds the Scotch even in habits, in external appearance, in accent. The arrogance of the English, which makes them aspire to be more perfect than the Scotch, goes further to smooth the way for the Pretender than a mutiny among the troops.

The French lady seemed surprised and pleased. Yet she exclaimed,

"What folly! What a blind fancy in your friends! Pray set aside these false presumptions which can lead to nothing but disappointment. No; nothing but a rising, nothing but force of arms can avail. Organize these! You must leave London now—"

"With you?"

"I will follow."

"Where?"

"To the garrison which you shall have won. To that nobleman's country-seat where you shall have prepared the levies, the raising of a force who shall stand armed at the moment in which the Queen draws her last breath."

"The Spaniards will send weapons."

"The Spaniards! When the parliamentary vessels which cover the canal carry all our. missives? Holland will not give us any help and Spain is powerless. The approach of ships to the west coast of England is almost impracticable, on account of the rocks. I ask of you, that you should tear yourself from the arms of your betrothed, should betake yourself to the north, seek to win over the garrisons in Aberdeen and Glasgow, and above all, prepare for a rising en masse in the Highlands. I myself will quit London on receipt of the first favourable intelligence which you send and will come—"

"To Edinburgh?"

"To Edinburgh."

Mutual understanding in a dangerous cause, a brightening gleam of success, the charm of a secret all his own, and the value which Sam saw placed on his courage and his energy, all these so carried him away that he dreamed himself freed from every fetter and overpowered the Parisian lady (who knew how to place a certain limit on her favours to him, and where to draw the line) with caresses to which she gave no check. It was as though he would carry away with him beforehand the reward for all that she expected him to do and all that he vowed himself ready to carry out. He drew her to his side, put his arm on her shoulder and covered her with passionate kisses, till, at length, she sprang up and pointed to the drawing-room from which at this moment a thunder of applause broke forth, in acknowledgment of a song, just ended, sung by the Italian, the melting strains of which had contributed in no small degree to excite Sam's wild extasies in the secret grotto. The audience in the saloon would now doubtless disperse and destroy the security of the *tête-à-tête*.

How warmly did Sam, hastening into the room, applaud the singer, of whose song he had heard nothing! How did he praise his execution, the quality of his voice, his rendering! All words spoken at random! And yet they sounded well-chosen. They were seconded by all present. Sam was at home in the disputes of that day between the musicians of Paris and Italy. Thus he disparaged Lully and extolled Handel. Thus he provoked a scene on the subject with Lord Lansdowne who on this occasion was really present, and would not allow either one or the other to be called in question, and proved himself throughout to be one of those pretended dilettantes in art whose words men are to deem oracular.

Sam seemed to be treading on air. He was amiability itself. He captivated everybody. At about one o'clock he put his arm within that of an officer of the Life guards and nodded a farewell, till early day, to Arthur Maxwell.

Maxwell regarded him with astonishment. He had perhaps been the only person who would have noticed Sam's absence during the singer's cantata, if he had not himself, in another way, been too much distracted from the beautiful song. He had merely stared straight before him, or sometimes looked absently at the gay colouring of the ceiling.

Sam had yet another crafty plan. He did not profess to be a gambler; but he now proposed to accompany the officers to a gaming room. Arthur, in passing, obtained this explanation of his staying out until morning. Little could the young man, who now betook himself quietly to his couch to dream of Ellinor, suspect that Sam had merely wished to have in him a witness for his declaration that he had forgotten himself, that he had played for a hundred crowns, and was in the greatest despair. His calculation was this, that old Robertson would release him from the obligations incurred by his word of honour given on this subject. He needed this sum of money in order to carry out Blanche's injunction to him to go to Scotland, to excite the garrisons to mutiny and prepare a land force.

When Arthur awoke the next morning and had dressed and was ready for breakfast, nothing was yet to be thought about Sam. The latter had indeed come home, but in rather disconsolate plight, so the servants said, by which they implied that he was intoxicated. Arthur breakfasted alone, went out, and paid his regular visit to Ellinor; for he could not permit this much-to-be-pitied girl to suffer still further deprivation.

They ordinarily talked on every subject, except about Sam. Nor did they talk of him on this day. Lord Arthur was a true friend. He spared Sam's character. Yet in his heart, he felt the gnawing reproach of loving his friend's betrothed. That Ellinor loved him in return, she had never confessed. But he had suspected it ever since he had seen her tearful eyes when once he had not come for some days; had not come for this reason, because he wished to keep down his feelings, to gain the mastery over himself.

It was not until the evening of this day that Maxwell saw his friend and companion. Maxwell was on his way to join Lady Nairn at supper (which meal gradually assumed the first rank among the five to which Englishmen, even at that day, were accustomed) when Sam met him with a disturbed countenance. He had missed his portfolio. He had not risen until noon and even then he had not immediately bethought him of the important place of concealment of his secrets. It was not until he was going out that he had sought with dismay for that which doubtless he had not brought home. He had rushed in haste to the gaming house which was kept by a Frenchman. The twice that he had staked he had been fortunate at play. His purse he had. The Frenchman did not put on a very complaisant air on hearing of his misfortune. "You always have good luck, Sir," said he. "You must have laid it down somewhere at home."

Sam followed the suggestion conveyed in these words, returned to Leicester Square, and hunted all over the staircases, passages, rooms, and cupboards. The portfolio was not to be found; nothing could be seen of Lady Nithsdale's letters, of Blanche's, nothing of his own plans, of his highly treasonable map so easy to be understood, nothing of Lord Carnwath's commentaries on his notes. If all these should fall into wrong hands, he would be lost; an accusation of felony when it could be proved, and here the proofs would be, cost a man his head. He ran to Lady Arabella's house in Grosvenor Square, and with every sign of alarm, he entreated permission of that lady to search her house. On receiving this, he hastened to the music hall, rushed into the grotto, but not a trace of his portfolio could he find.

Blanche was not in the house at the time. He waited for her return. When she came in, and declared that she knew nothing of it, and even became very angry at the possibility of his not having taken better care of a thing of so much importance, and plainly expressed her suspicion that Sam must have passed the night in bad company, and, on his silence, assumed an appearance of jealousy, half in earnest, half pretended, which prompted her to bang the door leading into her boudoir in his face and to lock it after her, then all his self-control forsook the strong man. The remembrance of yesterday's happiness seemed likewise lost. Sam could not vindicate himself, for this reason, that Lady Arabella was present. The latter assisted in the search, and suggested whether it might not he necessary that the conspirators, her son's friends, should he made acquainted with what had happened, so that all precautionary measures should be taken in case the papers should fall into the hands of the police. When the Countess intreated Blanche to open her door, the latter answered that she herself must prepare as far as possible for a flight which had now become necessary. And that Sam had, at all events, better conceal himself immediately, or better still, go away on a journey.

With this reply Sam quitted the ladies. He spoke

once more to the house servants, offered rewards and promised forgetfulness of the occurrence, if any one had dishonestly appropriated the portfolio and would preserve a faithful secrecy regarding what he had found, which was useless save to the owner. All in vain. Nothing was discovered which could calm his fears. Thus he returned to Lady Nairn's house, and in this frame of mind he stopped Maxwell before they went to the supper-table.

"Every mouthful will stick in my throat, till I get the confounded thing back into my possession," said he, when Maxwell recommended him to repeat the search, and at least not to excite his aunt about the affair, but at all events to bear himself like a man. For Sam was pale as death, and looked already like a convicted criminal.

He could have no need to search for the portfolio in Ellinor's house. He looked for it after supper, at which he did not eat a mouthful, and even in the streets, although it was night. He inquired at every place where he could recollect to have stopped. He inquired of the officers who lived on the opposite side of the Thames. In vain. How he cursed the quantity of wine which he had taken in the gaming house! He had only done this in memory of the scene in the grotto.

The friends debated whether old Robertson

should be made acquainted with this loss. Sam, uneasy as to the contents of the pocket-book, opposed this; but he gave his friend a vivid description of that which likewise weighed on him, his gaming debts. This story was all a deceit. Despair at his real loss aided the actor well in what he feigned.

"It was just this gambling debt which confused me, and made me forget everything else," said he. "I cannot delay longer than three days to pay the officers. From whom can I get six hundred crowns? My brother will not give them to me. It is only Ellinor, only Robertson," said the hypocrite (who merely saw in Ellinor a well of gold), correcting himself; "the old man alone can help me in this!"

Though Maxwell did not always think leniently of his friend, yet in this case, when the lost portfolio filled him also with anxious fears although he was hopeful throughout, he promised to take upon himself the office of mediator, and, whilst in Cavendish Street, only to touch upon the loss of the pocket-book so far as this might serve judiciously to aid the cause of Sam's repentance, of his sorrow for having gambled away so much money, and assurances of his amendment.

But before Maxwell could find a favourable opportunity for carrying out this kind project, Sam had himself betrayed the importance of his loss by the uneasiness which he made evident. During these days he only came once to see Ellinor, and then he showed the distraction of his mind more plainly than ever. If a knock were heard at the house-door, he started up. He seemed well satisfied that her father was said to be ill. Thus he avoided the sharp, scrutinizing looks of the old man, whose behaviour to him had for some time been growing cooler and cooler.

The anxieties which prevailed in Lady Arabella's house and with Blanche regarding the lost notebook, were increased when all who heard of it advised against a public declaration of the loss and an announcement of the address, where any one finding the papers, at once so valueless and so important, might deliver them.

The inquiries which were made at Lord Nairn's house, whether anything had yet been discovered respecting the absence of the missing book, increased Maxwell's and Sam's anxiety to fever pitch. At length the former fully shared in Sam's opinion that he had best conceal himself or, indeed, if he could obtain sufficient means from old Robertson, betake himself immediately to the North. On points of opinion with regard to the public affairs of Great Britain, the friends were of the same mind.

It was on the third evening after Lady Arabella's

brilliant party that Sam declared to his friend, that he could no longer endure this state of dread and of responsibility to Blanche and to so many other persons. Maxwell must endeavour to come to some clear understanding with old Robertson, at least as regarded his gambling debts. Ellinor had already remarked that something of importance was weighing on the minds of the friends. She had joined together in her mind the gambling debt first spoken of and the loss of the note-book which was confessed afterwards, and she said, she was sure that Sam must have played away a very considerable sum of money. She had already made her father, who became more and more unwell, acquainted with Lord Maxwell's anxieties. Sam did not doubt but that Maxwell would be his most skilful and effectual mediator with the old man.

He accompanied his friend to Cavendish Street and said, that he would wait at "The Pitcher without a handle" for Maxwell's return. The speech which Sam had made with knavish wrinkling of his eyebrows: "If he refuses now, then I will bring down upon him our discovery on the betrothal night like—a flying horse! This will bring him down!" had imbued Maxwell with feelings of the most lively indignation.

It was a mild night in spring. The air had not only that soft balminess, which seems to incite all the re-awakening life of nature to put forth bud and leaf and to struggle again against winter, which is being chased away; but the fragrance of flowers already penetrated through the impure atmosphere of the large city, coming from numerous gardens, from many a large park in the neighbourhood, and from the garden of Bedlam, for the pleasure grounds of the lunatics were not far distant. Many open spots also were planted with flowers. Ellinor had at her home a piece of garden, which she had already made to look green with currant bushes, such favourites in England.

Sam might have waited for half an hour with Mr. and Mrs. Oakins, when Maxwell made his appearance and whispered to him,

"I think all will go well. But the old man wishes to speak to you himself."

At this announcement Sam was calmed and rose.

"Where did you find him?" he asked, fixing his eyes upon some men who had come into the tavern after himself, and who seemed to him to be objects of suspicion; since, as he maintained, they had scanned him from head to foot and were still talking in whispers about him.

Maxwell saw the nervous glances which Sam

cast at that corner of the alehouse in which these men were sitting, and said with a smile:

"Have you already begun to see ghosts again? It is only that they are astonished at your dress, which is better than what they are accustomed to see here. For the rest," he continued, as they left the tavern, "I can tell you that old John is ill, he has been so these three days; but he received me, listened quietly to all, shook his head several times, and asked how much you had lost?"

"You told him—"

"I was in some perplexity; the old man looked at me with penetrating eyes; and was cold even towards me to-day."

"That vexed you and so you betrayed me."

"Was it betrayal to tell him that you had lost a considerable sum?"

"And how many guineas will he advance?"

"You must come to him yourself. Prepare yourself for reproaches! Only take them quietly, do not answer angrily. Promise me this, or I will slay you here on this very spot; do you understand? Respect his secrets, even if he does not spare yours. Ellinor is at this moment standing at the window, with a beating heart, and praying for a prosperous termination to the interview."

Sam went with his friend. It was still light. The evening glow was fading into moonlight.

He stood for a moment at the nearest corner, to assure himself that the men who had scrutinized him so closely were not following. They had indeed left the house, but had turned in another direction without looking round at him.

"Who knows what old hag may not have found the note-book?" said Maxwell. "Its contents will long ago have done good service in wrapping up butter and cheese."

"I would not wish," answered Sam, "that you had seen the looks which the solicitor in Clerkenwell cast on me as I passed him to-day, when I went there for my brother who has inherited some lawsuits from my grandfather with the rest of his property. It seemed as though he would say, 'I am just come from the Lieutenant of the Tower and I am surprised that your Honor is walking about at large.' People are watching me, of this I am certain. They wish to see who those are who are concerned in the contents of my note-book."

Arthur Maxwell did not contradict this. He was aware also of the danger of his own position; and above all, he hoped that Sam might obtain the means to go away from London with all possible speed.

"Miss Ellinor is in the garden, sir!" said Miss Kitty to the visitors and especially to Sir Samuel Mordaunt. "Her father has sent her there, I do not know whether until you should come or until you shall have gone away."

This witticism only called forth a forced laugh from Sam.

There was still quite light enough left for sauntering about the garden. We might say of this little green space that it was not large and was devoid of taste. At that time, these little gardens with flowerbeds bordered with box, clipped hedges and a little crag of pieces of rock piled up together, between which in the summer were pots filled with iris, and which at this season had tulips blooming among them, were considered to be most charming and attractive. The paths were strewn with bright yellow sand. But everywhere all was natural green and not artificial that grew here. Neither knife nor shears had been able to destroy the colour or the fragrance of that portion of the natural growth which they had left.

Ellinor came in some agitation to meet her friend. She said in a strange tone, that her father had sent her into the garden, because he was waiting for Sam in his apartments which, indeed, opened partially upon the garden but were protected from inquisitive listeners by strong shutters, which were now closed.

Arthur remained behind with Ellinor, whilst Sam went to old Robertson's room.

Within the same walls, closed in on all sides, in which Sam had a few months ago received the promise of Ellinor's hand, he now found the old man who though coughing, had on Sam's knock answered with a very audible "Come in!"

"You find me suffering a good deal," began the old gentleman, when Sam entered and had taken the offered seat. "The Spring always tries me the most. She would fain make their departure to a better world easy to the aged. In London spring carries off more people than the hardest winter. God has ordained it so. Thus we may die in full hope and anticipation—"

Sam murmured some words which were meant to sound like deprecating the application of such opinions to the speaker. On this day, he observed more attentively the room, which presented a calm peaceful appearance. The furniture was simple. The sofa, on which he sat, had a green silk covering. The table covers, and carpet were green; the curtains, which were now drawn, were also green. A lamp hung from the ceiling. If Sam had been a few inches taller, he might have knocked his head against the frame of a picture representing Mary Wilson, Ellinor's mother, in life size. An artistically wrought time-piece ticked on the table in front of him. The old man's writing-table was covered with books and papers. His treasures, Sam thought, were probably contained in the cupboards, the key-holes of which could easily be discerned on the hangings which were likewise green. Robertson was in his house-dress. He wore a black velvet cap on his head. On his feet were high slippers which Ellinor had embroidered for him.

"I hear that you have had losses at play," he began, without seating himself, and indeed pacing up and down, a token of how much he was agitated, notwithstanding his apparent composure.—"How can a man give himself up to such habits!"

Sam, who although he had played, had won, heaved a sigh and bore himself like one who is possessed of an unfortunate propensity but who, nevertheless, has an earnest desire to amend.

But he said, "Ah, Father John, did you never gamble?"

The old man stood still, and gazed inquiringly at the speaker.

"I mean as a merchant," continued Sam, who was almost terrified at having assumed the appearance of again wishing to drive Mr. Robertson into a corner about his mysteries, whereby he might perhaps meet with opposition rather than compliance from "little Lobster" who was sometimes very inflexible. He quite intended to obey Maxwell's urgent injunction on this point. "As a merchant, Sir," he continued; "such as you were formerly. You used then to fit out ships, and you left it to wind and weather to decide whether they should bring you gain or loss. Indeed, whilst waiting to see whether the event would disappoint your hopes, you even took a more favourable view of success than reason warranted. You kept yourself scathless in case of misfortune, and by fixing a certain price defrauded the poor, who had nothing to do with your good, or bad fortune."

"That is a necessity," replied the old man, calmly, "to which self-preservation compels us under the fickle moods of fortune. Also, it would seem as if God had so willed it that the stronger should, on earth, boldly make use of his advantages. But a gambler tries by a guilty industry to make amends for the true strength that he lacks. He wishes to win in a moment that on which others must spend years and even more. Besides, gambling is a folly for this reason, that the real winnings remain in the hands of the man who keeps the table, and who laughs in his sleeve because he can carry on his battle in the world whilst all you others are soon tired out. Why it is, that gamblers always have bad principles as regards everything in life, I do not know. But so it is."

Sam had no need for much dissembling when he answered that he had only been the victim of a rash moment.

"Because there are societies," continued Robertson, in a heightened tone, "into which an unfortunate inclination of wishing to shine draws you. Repress this inclination! I know well that this longing is on the verge of bringing you to ruin—"

"How? You know?" said Sam, trying by an assumed smile to represent the fears of the old man as groundless, and at the same time to conceal his own anxiety.

"Sam! Sam!" proceeded the old gentleman with increasing excitement. "I seize on this moment to warn you of the abyss over which you are walking. Do not forget that I have given into your hands all that is dearest to me on earth, my child. I would not that she should fall into destruction with you."

"Father Robertson!" cried Sam in a gentler tone and as if hurt; and yet he felt strangely that the old man spoke as though he (Sam) were standing before the court of justice which he so much feared.

"Do not call me by that name unless you deserve to do so," was Robertson's added warning. "Do not deceive the tenderness and affection which induced me to listen to the wishes of your deceased grandfather."

"Only Will Mordaunt's wishes?" asked Sam in measured tones, which did not belie the malice of his question.

"What then could have induced me to give him peace, during what proved alas! to be the short remaining portion of his life, and to give it him to carry to the grave, if it were not the hope that your intellect, the acquirements with which you are so richly endowed, would contribute to refine your mind and to preserve you from the ensnarements of the great world? Alas! there is in you nothing but inclination for all that is most unprofitable, for the thriving weeds of hypocrisy and dissimulation."

"Sir! You assuredly know right well why you entertained such kindly feelings towards Will Mordaunt!"

These bitter, threatening words, which were accompanied by a chilling smile, were to the old man, as was intended, like a dagger, like a shining, deadly weapon half-drawn from its sheath.

And at them, Robertson started. He looked nervously on one side, scanned the bold speaker with a hasty glance, was silent, and seemed to be obliged to recover himself from the effect of such knavish malice in the heart of the man who made this random guess.

However he said in a confidential tone to Sam, who scrutinized the old man's features inquiringly and enjoyed the effect of his words with a feeling of triumph:

"Sam, I hear too, that you have had another misfortune."

Sam, not unjustly, looked upon the apparent gentleness of these words as a counter-weapon presented at himself. For although they sounded sympathetic, yet they had in them a ring as though they would express:

"You wish to represent me as in the power of your grandfather and yourself. I will show you, for once, the power I have over you!"

And indeed when Sam, startled, remained silent, the old man came up close to him and continued:

"Sam! Boy! you have lost your note-book, and you tremble lest it should have been found! Found perhaps by some Englishman who loves his rightful king, his pure, gospel, faith?"

Sam sprang up. Dissimulation was no longer

of use. The importance of truth fell too fearfully on his heart. He groaned, drew his breath audibly, and in vain made an effort to say more than; "Ah —let—leave that—"

"But I shall not leave it!" cried Robertson in a marked and piercing voice. "God may perhaps one day have mercy upon those who are guilty of high treason. But here on earth, worldly justice and the anger of our nation bring them to the gallows!"

Sam supported himself by the arm of the sofa. His strength, his disdain, the power of his malice, all had left him.

"If you were but on the way thither alone," the old man went on, "a traitor to your country, the ravens should be welcome to croak after you to Tyburn Hill! But the honour of another man is bound up in you, of a man who has given you the dearest thing he has on earth, his unfortunate child, a maiden who, by such a disgrace, would see her innocent heart sacrificed, her pure, pious, loving nature trampled upon! Shall she be suffered to weep for a criminal, a deceiver?"

Sam stood trembling. For tears had risen to the eyes of the old man himself. Sam was coming nearer to him. He stretched out his hand towards the terrible censor—

"Touch me not!" cried the grey headed man.

"Take your hand from near me, the hand that could write words of treason. Treasonable also to the obligations of your betrothal! Are you trembling, villain, for the letters which may be found written by a daughter of hell, by a woman who has let France loose, let Antichrist loose on England's isle, in order to bring hearts to destruction in this land, to lure away renegades from their fealty, and yourself, above all, from the oath which you swore to my child when you placed the ring on her finger?"—

"Sir, Sir," stammered Sam, his lips standing open and stiff. For thus, thus, no one could speak but one who was acquainted with the contents of the note-book, who perhaps even had it in his possession!

"Oh! my poor child!" groaned the old man. "Deceived by a wretch who stole his way into my confidence, who wanted to get from me the means to please the fancies of Italian mistresses!"

Quite in opposition to the words with which under other circumstances Sam Mordaunt would have replied to this accusation, he now extended his hands towards John Robertson as if imploring help. The tone in which the latter had spoken had expressed all too clearly; "I obtained my knowledge of your want of truth from the selfsame spring for which you are searching in such despair."

"Father John! I swear to you—Trust my words! God Almighty is witness to my vow that I never, never again—But—" he stopped, already interrupting his agitation of fear, of hope, of joy, by a regard for his prudent calculations and dissimulations; "but who told you that your unjust accusation—"

"Silence!" cried the old man interrupting him in a sonorous voice, and stretching towards Heaven his arm which, with hand and forefinger extended, he then allowed to sink slowly, pointing the while towards the ground, as though he would say; "There, down there, on your knees at my feet, is your proper place!"

With this, and whilst Sam, utterly annihilated, remained silent and followed the movements of the old man with his stiffened eyeballs, the latter walked to his writing-table, drew a long breath as though thus to obtain new courage and new strength, and drew out one of the drawers.

Sam's anxious glance immediately discovered that a black object lying in the opened drawer was none other than—his note-book.

He rushed towards it. Robertson quietly allowed him to seize the portfolio. With trembling hands, Sam unfastened the straps, looked into the inner pocket of this imprisoned holder of his secrets, found all the letters of the conspirators, Blanche's letters, the map of Great Britain, all just as they were before. He broke into a convulsive laugh of joy, and of relief from a load which had weighed fearfully on his mind.

When the old man also gave him a purse of gold for defraying his gambling debts, Sam was overcome with emotions called forth from his better self. He would have returned the purse but could not find words in which to do so, for joy deprived him of speech. He kissed the old man's hands, and overpowered him with demonstrations of tenderness which, under other circumstances, would have made no one more happy than this old gentleman; but which now only served to increase the oppression on his heart and to fill him with an unconquerable melancholy regarding the sad prospects for his later days, which stood before him as certainties.

"That, for the traitor!" he said, pointing to the note-book; and then again putting the purse from his own hands into those of Sam, "this, for the gambler!"

"But where," at length broke from Sam's lips, when he had put the note-book quickly into his pocket, and was still holding the purse in his hand, "but how did you, dear father, little Lobster, dear, sweet, little Crabbie, how did you come by my unfortunate documents?"

In return for this, in Robertson's frame of mind, thoroughly ill-timed joking, the old man remained cold as ice, raised his left arm and pointed to the door.

But when Sam, after pocketing the purse likewise, still did not seem to choose to understand this intimation to him to leave the room, and began instead to ask afresh and in a different, and dubiously inquiring tone; "But for Heaven's sake, Sir, what angel was it who brought the thing to your house?" then old Robertson opened the door himself, took hold of a button of Sam's coat, and led the astonished man out. Sam only heard that the old man then locked himself into his room.

At this moment he gave himself up to one sole feeling, that of joy at his regained security, which, like a dammed up stream when the flood gates are let loose, poured forth in a torrent over his soul. He rushed to the garden where in the moonlight which cast its magic rays around the gloomy walls, causing these to throw shadows grave and gay over the garden, Arthur and Ellinor were strolling, engaged in anxious conversation: he pressed Ellinor (who looked as though awaking from a dream) to his breast, covered her cheeks with kisses and excited the greatest astonishment in both his betrothed and his friend by his behaviour, the reason for which he but very imperfectly explained.

It was not until Arthur was alone with Sam, who had taken leave of Ellinor with the tenderest assurances and protestations of a speedy return, that the latter heard of the almost fabulous good fortune which had befallen the enviable possessor of Ellinor's hand.

CHAPTER IX.

The Death of the Queen.

A CHANGE for the better did really seem to come over Sam Mordaunt. His visits to Robertson's house grew more frequent and were of longer duration than formerly. The father's grave demeanour relaxed. He saw with satisfaction that Sam was making earnest preparations for enrolling himself on the list of London barristers and for placing himself at the disposal of those who might require his aid. An English barrister is obliged, when called to the bar, to take an oath of allegiance to the crown. When Robertson reminded Sam of this, and half jesting, half vexed, said that the probability was that Sam would hesitate to bind himself to be a loyal subject to the queen, Sam made as though all political objects and disputes were now far from his thoughts. And indeed, so it appeared. The Viscountess de Champfleury had betaken herself, by a circuitous route, to Paris for some time. The parting scene between her Ladyship and Sam, which had taken place at Southampton whither he had accompanied her, was unknown even to Arthur Maxwell. Sam had returned from his excursion, of the object of which Arthur was ignorant, with an assurance which lent him strength for carrying on his work of dissimulation towards Ellinor and her father.

Now, at length, Sam's keen eyes perceived that Ellinor did not love him, and seemed to live for Arthur alone. His knowledge of the world should have made him discover this sooner. But at first, he explained the interest which Ellinor always openly showed in Arthur, by the idea that this was founded on the feeling that it was due to one who loved him and was loved by him in return. Now he perceived that Ellinor's coldness when he was alone with her, and her excitement when Arthur came in, must be attributed to some other cause. Mean as was his entire nature, this discovery was accompanied by the thought; "How may not this be productive of consequences disadvantageous to yourself?" With Robertson's sentiments which had no doubt become suspicious towards himself, might not the lovers get the better of the old man's resolutions and expect Sam to withdraw his claims? At how high a price then, such was now his calculation, at how high a price can you sell your claims? This reckoning he made with perfect calmness. He would derive some advantage if he were to receive the sum which Robertson would then owe him immediately, and not be obliged to wait for the old man's death. The acquisition of a wife who, after all, would be a drag upon his freedom of action and who would torment him with her jealousy and with scenes of discontent, did not appear to him very enviable. Indeed his demoniacal mind, devoid of all feelings of true honour, of all honour on moral subjects, led him, whilst he laughed and stared like a satyr, to imagine a marriage in which his wife had married him without love, and his friend should take his place and thus be slavishly bound to him and owe him things of far more importance in his eyes than conjugal happiness and honour. The road he set before him led to the highest offices of the state. To find himself in the peerage at the close of his career, to receive knighthood from the future sovereign, James the Third, to become a cabinet minister, these were the objects of his highest ambition. Lord Maxwell could rise by his own family connexions. An inheritance, title, office were all before him. If Maxwell were bound to him (thus ran his ambitious, but as regards true ambition, his mean thoughts), "then the fits of independence in which the boy sometimes now threatens to break away from my influence would no longer take place." Besides, he could not for a moment believe that Arthur could be in earnest and think of marrying the daughter of a man who held an inferior, and indeed a doubtful position in society. Sometimes he would watch with sardonic smiles, and a cynical air, outbursts of the feeling which existed in Ellinor's heart for his friend; then he would take up the flowers which Lord Arthur had sent to her, would explain the meaning which was probably intended to lie in the each flower selected, and ask for messages for the "kind boy." When he saw the annoying effect this had upon Ellinor, he put on hypocritical fits of a jealousy which he certainly never felt as regarded her. His heart throbbed for the French woman alone, with whom he carried on an unbroken correspondence. On quitting Southampton harbour, she had again given him assurances of her favour, which made him return from thence in a wild tumult of excitement.

Ellinor suffered inexpressibly. Her love for Arthur was combined with most oppressive thoughts. Connected with them were ideas which are unknown in our day. Just as our mode of thought and our perceptions have freed our bodies from whalebone and steels, so they have also freed us from the rules of tradition regarding family honour and religious compulsion by conscience. A promise made to a father, a contract proclaimed to the world, these were held more sacred then than they are now.

It was necessary for modern thinkers to step in and to inculcate, and understand how to prove alluringly, that there is a tribunal within our own breast whose judgment ought to prevail, even though the consequences form critical exceptions to prevalent and pernicious rules. The law of nature and of free, unfettered feeling can only be established on the ruined black marble tables of opinions rendered sacred by antiquity.

For a long time Ellinor did not call that which made her inmost heart happy, love. She called her rejoicings, when Arthur came once more after remaining away for a long time, sins. Hot tears fell from her eyes when he went away, but they fell on her book of prayers, where she sought out the places in which prayers were addressed to God for pardon for a disinclination to walk in His laws. She went to church and allowed the stern moralists of the times to make her very bones and marrow quiver, and listened to the punishments of Eternal Justice on all that was, from the pulpit, denominated wandering affections, pride and wicked coquetry with a clear conviction that she herself would be cast into the fires of destrustion to languish for relief. Then she would totter from her seat into the open air, wishing to believe herself reconciled with God; and see! Maxwell would meet her and complain that the sermon had been so long, and that he had been so long obliged to restrain his impatience for their return home. Then she felt again as though she were floating through a garden of roses, and as if her spirit had wings like those of the lovely children round the organ (thus she consoled herself) who strewed lovely flowers about in the world, and if one observed aright, could not with long trompets of judgment really cause alarm to either dead or living.

In the already much troubled state of her father's mind, this mental conflict in his child first assumed the perceptible form of a care, which grew upon him and seemed almost to demand an admonition and stringent sentence on his child, on one day when Lord Arthur disappeared from London without coming to take leave. He had left his farewell to Ellinor in writing.

"Ellinor," thus he wrote, "I leave the tranquillity of my heart behind me in that quiet little room, in which I discovered the entrance to Paradise. Yes! all those who have been in India may tell me that there alone, beneath the blooming mango tree, is the entrance to Paradise. Even the chattering watchman of the Indies was not wanting in the little room where all was a palm-grove, all unchanging blue sky for me."—

Ellinor looked at Bab, her gay Brazilian bird to whom this allusion referred. She wept so bitterly that her father could not really be angry with her in his heart and he foiled the curiosity of Miss Kitty who became too confidential to him on the affairs of the house and soon, as always in such cases happened with his domestics, received of her dismissal. He referred Ellinor to religion, which teaches us self-renunciation under such circumstances. He dwelt upon his own past life to her, on the fortitude of her mother when he lost the prospect of a fortunate lot in life in Uncle Buck's bond. And when Ellinor would have replied with the title and refrain of the play, "No magic like Love," he raised his eyes to Heaven and said;

"In every trial of life, the goodness of God ordains something by which we find compensation for it! Only have patience, my child! This will be made plain also to you!"

Of his other grief, that Arthur Maxwell had doubtless gone to the North in the interests of the Jacobite conspirators, he was never able to speak to his child. Alas! he had found it impossible to disabuse the young man of the idea, which at that time possessed nearly the whole of the English nobility, really blinding them in their notions of legitimate right, of the Divine favour, and of necessary expiation for the execution of Charles the First.

In the height of the summer of the same year, on the 1. August 1714, Queen Anne died. The Jacobite conspiracy broke out immediately. Immediately after the black flag was hoisted on St. James' Palace, Sam Mordaunt went away to Scotland.

This is not the place in which to describe the course of this remarkable revolution which resulted in the complete victory of the popular party, of Protestantism and of the succession resolved on by Parliament. George Louis, the Elector of Hanover, came to England; dismissed, even before his entrance into London, two equivocal ministers, whom his predecessor had left in office, recalled the Duke of Marlborough to the head of the army, and ordered the insurrection which had begun to show itself in Scotland, to be suppressed by reliable generals, experienced in the art of war. This did not, at first, meet with full success.

Lord Mar had stired up the Highlands to revolt, several regiments and garrisons were won over. A militia force was raised and led against the royal troops who, indeed, at first suffered some reverses. The utter incapacity of the Pretender (who landed on the shores of Great Britain amid a train of adores, male and female) did not, however, act favourably on the first promising and hopeful signs of success to his cause.

His followers were beaten in two inconsiderable engagements. All fled together. James the Third himself made his escape. He was obliged to take precautions lest the price set upon his head, which had been doubled by the Parliament and now amounted to £200,000, should tempt any to earn it.

The punishment which fell upon the conspirators was fearful. King George, by nature indolent and coldhearted, allowed what would to happen. His minister, Robert Walpole, pointed out to him that an act of national life must here be carried out by the English among themselves. It was a question of a struggle of annihilation, Tories or Whigs, as formerly the red or the white rose; or at least, the conclusion of a period of constant disquiet, constant disturbance of internal peace, which had now, in the lapse of time and in the cause of true national interests, taken up different aims from that of gratifying the ambition of a princely family, which had outlived its day. Capital punishments must strike terror, in cannon-balls for the mutinous military, hanging for revolutionists and meddlers with the civil power, and the sword of the executioner for nobler heads.

Immediately after the battle of Preston all officers, who had gone over and who were caught, were shot. In Lancashire twenty-two and in London four civilians were hung. Seven of the Scottish leaders of highest rank were sent to the Tower. Lord Kenmure and James Earl of Derwentwater, the young son of Lady Arabella Ratcliffe, were immediately executed. Lord Nithsdale was saved by his wife who, when she visited him in the Tower, dressed herself in his clothes and made him escape in hers by that field of blood in English Chronicles, the Tower Hamlets. Lords Widdrington, Wintoun, Carnwath and Nairn (Arthur Maxwell's own uncle) were in the Tower awaiting the announcement of their executions, which were only delayed for the purpose of confronting these noblemen with, and obtaining evidence against other persons. The voice of the minority in Parliament and of some of the weekly publications, above all that of the noble and talented Richard Steele (friend of the poet, Richard Savage, who died so prematurely) desiring milder treatment had not as yet prevailed.

Among those under sentenced of hanging in Lancashire, was Samuel Mordaunt. The "man of the future" died on the gallows. On Lord Arthur, who was taken prisoner as an officer, sentence of death by shooting was passed.

* * * * *
* * * * *

A year had almost elapsed since the day on which Ellinor Robertson had received Arthur Maxwell's farewell letter. All was silent around her as she sat in her corner-room, once so cheerful. The Indian bird was no longer living. Perhaps he had not been able to bear the suffocating air of London, perhaps had not had his natural food, or he may have been neglected in the days of horror and alarm, in those days in which one might even have appealed to the dumb walls for sympathy. Nor was Miss Kitty any longer in the house. She had been recommended by the old gentleman to a duchess, who was intending to visit Italy, as travelling-companion, because she understood French. Mr. Conybeare, the clerk at Doctors' Commons had offered the situation. Kitty had been sent away with handsome presents.

Ellinor sat there in deep grief. She had a spinning wheel before her, and spun now and then. Machines in Birmingham and Manchester had not yet superseded the work of the human hand. It was a bright day. In London, as elsewhere, the sun of late autumn is that most be depended on. It shines so certainly there that one may feel sure that it remains almost absent during the other seasons.

Its evening rays seemed to gleam cheerfully on the still, mournful life around. The engravings, the books of travels, all now were gilded by it, though undisturbed. Indeed, nothing but weekly papers, handbills, and government notices under a weight, a sleeping dog made of bronze, lay upon the centre table which was covered with a black cloth, as though everything which surrounded Ellinor were to be in mourning. The monthly roses, amid which she sat at the window, alone wore the hues which had formerly bloomed on Ellinor's cheeks.

Those cheeks were now blanched. Round her eyes were light red circles. They told of injury to the beautiful blue stars, which had wept so much during these sad times that they could no longer be relieved by tears. Yes, indeed, Ellinor had wept even for Sam's fearful death. People had come in and had declared that she lay in motionless despair. Her betrothed on the gallows! Hung like a common thief or murderer! The feeling among the families of those friends of her father who have been more often spoken of, could not be restrained by circumstances which might, perhaps, soften Eleanor's grief. Neither had they any doubts in their judgment of Sam's character such as the bride, who seemed on every account worthy of pity, had long had in her own heart.

Yet in a certain way, Eleanor was affected even to despair by the freedom from her engagement. The more that that inward demon, who in old times was called the devil, said to her, "Rejoice that you are now free from him," so much the more did she conscientiously dwell upon the hideous manner in which this had happened, pictured to herself the last hours of this proud, bold man with all his mental and physical sufferings, and met all the demonstrations of condolence to which she had to listen with sincerity and without any dissimulation. Alas! not infrequently fate vouchsafes compensation, which far exceeds the measure of that which we have expected and which, instead of cheering us, rather oppresses and shames us.

But why in truth should she not despair? The life of their dear friend Lord Arthur Maxwell was also threatened; her visitors blamed him also. Not only because they thought the views of the Jacobites altogether godless, but also because they considered these young noblemen (Lady Arabella's son who had been beheaded was only twenty four years of age) to have mis-led others and especially the hopeful Sam Mordaunt. The only sign of sympathy which the Rev. Thomas Mordaunt, who had now been removed to a larger town, showed to the Robertson family on the fearful end of his brother was an execration of his brother's noble friends and particularly of this Arthur Maxwell who stood especially noted in all the proscription lists. The clerical gentleman wished him the same end as that of his own brother, only that the gallows should be a few yards higher. The intelligence that Arthur Maxwell also had been caught, and had been shot by sentence of a court-martial, might on any day appear in the handbills which were looked for with fearful anxiety and hastily bought as soon as they appeared. The fact of his not having made use of his commission could not protect him from the consequences which his peculiar position in this instance would bring with it.

The shades of twilight were falling deeper and deeper over the streets. It was growing darker and darker. Ellinor's father had returned home from a walk which he had taken in order to breathe the fresh air. At first these events had prostrated him. But when he saw that Ellinor needed his whole support he roused himself, ordered the coachman Twistle to harness his horses and Mr. Pipperton to bring his sedans more frequently, and displayed a marked firmness. As a patriot, he forgot his personal grief and judged as the voice of the people judged. His dislike of Samuel Mordaunt gave him strength, a dislike which Ellinor could not feel so heartily as her father.

In order to distract his child's mind, her father talked, at the lonely meals of which they now partook, of what he had seen and heard during his walks which had now begun to take the place of drives and rides in sedans. On this day, he told anecdotes of children whom he had seen at play, of bold riders, of the throng that stopped up the streets, of many old acquaintances whom he had met. He told her all the news that had been received from the colonies and from the continent, of the death of Louis XIV. and of the new state of things under the Prince Regent, which would scarcely be an improvement as regarded France, but would be advantageous to England, as the Regent did not share in Louis XIV.'s hatred of England. Nor did they fail to speak of the hot disputes on their native English ground, of the ungenerous use which had been made of the victory won over the Jacobites, which displayed itself especially in the change of certain forms in the parliamentary constitution.

When the time came to retire to rest and Robertson, according to his habit, was going down to his room on the ground floor with a light in his hand after giving his child an affectionate kiss, he heard a loud knock at the house door together with that clang, which still in London supplies the place of the house-bell.

"Who is there?" inquired the old man who went himself to the door and who, cautious at all times, was doubly so in these days of military rule.

"Open to me, Sir," was the answer, in a low tone but clearly distinguishable, spoken through the key-hole.

"Who are you?" asked Robertson perplexed. The danger of a sudden attack by thieves was not impossible, at all events in this part of the town.

"A friend," was the reply; and when Robertson still did not turn the key which was in the lock, the voice outside continued,

"Thank God that you are at the door yourself and not any of your servants. Open it for old friendship's sake."

"It is Lord Arthur," said Robertson, trembling with joy and anxiety. He raised his arm, in order indeed to open the door, but it seemed to have lost its power through terror. The voice sounded in his ears exactly like that of his old friend.

He indeed it was. He stood before the old man in the dress of a common workman. A large cocked-hat almost concealed his whole face, which was covered with a beard. His high waterman's boots might have made him pass for a dock labourer or perhaps for a sailor. He embraced the old man who had put his light on the floor, and had the presence of mind to extinguish it with his foot. For, from the basement where the servants were still awake, voices and steps were heard approaching, urged by the heavy knocks at the house-door at so late an hour.

Lord Arthur felt himself hurriedly pushed into Robertson's room. He heard the old man's voice calling down the kitchen stairs, "All is right!" And then he fell, exhausted, into the arms of the man in whose house he had found succour and shelter.

"Where do you come from?" asked Robertson.

"From Lancashire," was the almost voiceless reply, which told so much.

"Did you see Sam before his death?"

It was some moments before Lord Arthur could answer. Then he said;

"After that day at Preston—all were scattered."

"But you know—"

"I know it. And Sam's fate will also be mine, if they find me. The wrath of the victor is implacable."

"Take courage!" said the old man, leading the fugitive, who threatened to break down altogether, in the dark to a seat on which he could recline. He then brought in the candle which had been left outside, lighted it again, fastened the door and looked closely at the young man whose disguise could not serve to conceal his imposing height and aristocratie mien.

"You are hungry," said Robertson, as Arthur lay breathless and exhausted.

The young man, who was prostrated as much by his feelings as by bodily weakness, shook his head which he had had closely cropped, took a piece of bread from his pocket and explained that it was not hunger which had thus overpowered him.

"But you need some other, better food! I will call Ellinor. She is still awake! All can be done quietly."

"Ellinor!" said Arthur with a deep sigh. "Then is not her heart broken?"

"By your farewell a year ago, that indeed might almost have broken it. By your peril of death—! But God will preserve you. When you are concerned we will not fear the punishment threatened to those who give shelter to the king's enemies. But why have you committed such follies? Why do you thus trouble your country?"

"My country is Scotland!" said Arthur with excitement. "And I was bound by a vow I had made! But let that pass! Other days will yet come!"

"Nay, not for the followers of the Pope!" cried Robertson raising his right arm and with prophetic mien. Then he folded his hands and said: "Bless them that curse you. Do good to them who have done you evil. Whether this man or that wear England's crown, you can never for that reason cease to be to us a fellowman, a brother! Ah, and you know it well, you were even more to me—a son! a son! And a father's heart receives even a prodigal son! Alas! that the unhappy man, put to so ignominious a death, has not come with you! His misfortunes would have improved him."

When John Robertson after this, repeated that he would call Ellinor so that the fainting man might at least partake of some hot tea, the latter entreated his friend to leave him in quiet for this night, and to wait until morning to disturb Ellinor with the news of his presence—"To delight her, to make her happy with it," interrupted her father; thinking, if all in the house can but be prepared for it and any sort of pretext can be found by which he may be represented to be a relation. "But," said Arthur, interrupting himself, "Kitty will recognise me! She will betray me!"

"She is no longer with us," said Robertson, calming him. "Those who are now about us do not know you. You can be my nephew, son of a brother of my sainted Mary, who has just arrived from India, or from Canada where the backwoodsmen wear a dress just like yours. First then, how did you escape from your pursuers? where do you come from?"

"Escape, Father John!" said Arthur, with a bitter laugh. "The runners are on my track. O how calm and peaceful is all within your house! But I fear, the time of rest is but short for me. Walpole's hirelings have blood-hounds that serve them well. They have tracked me from the Tyne to London. At night I made my way over fields and hedges. Often the runners were in front of me. Then they crossed me, when they turned back. Not even at the gates of London, no, not until I reached the streets did they lose my track. It is possible that they may surround this quarter of the town and discover me, notwithstanding your vigilance. I have not slept for seven nights. In the daytime I crept into the woods (which, thanks to the end of summer, have shed their leaves so opportunely) that I might bury myself under the dead leaves so as not to be seen. There I slept through many dangers."

"And do the same now!" said the old man, preparing a bed.

The exhaustion of the fugitive and his need of rest were so great that he wanted nothing but to undress, to be provided with clean linen and taken to a bed.

Collecting all his strength and presence of mind, Robertson rendered the assistance which his compassionate heart suggested, and had the happiness of seeing the unexpected comer stretched on his host's bed without any opposition, and of hearing him falling gently asleep.

But for himself, Robertson could get no rest. More than half an hour had passed since he had given Ellinor his farewell kiss. He might have supposed her already asleep. Yet when he had assured himself that the overwearied traveller had sunk into a heavy slumber, he went upstairs to the higher story and knocked at Ellinor's door. She was still sitting on her bed in a reverie, though half undressed.

Her father was obliged to repress the exclamations of surprise and joy which broke from Ellinor when she heard his news. A newly-engaged companion slept in a neighbouring room. Ellinor's father reminded her of the caution which must be exercised, and of the peril not yet overcome. He said to his child that they would agree to call this nocturnal visitor a nephew of his, a cousin of Ellinor's, who had arrived from Canada and who was a trader in timber. He would immediately himself quietly put better clothes by his bedside.

Lord Arthur Maxwell in the house! The tender, affectionate friend whom she had believed utterly lost! The warmly-loved friend whose attractions had only been rightly acknowledged when he was no longer visible to the being who had in him alone found happiness and peace, for whom alone she had felt esteem, and all the mystic, secret, feelings of love, when his gentle voice, which so easily hushed all the storms of life, was no longer audible to her ears! Arthur Maxwell here! Surrounded by dangers! But was it not some angel from heaven who had led him hither amid darkness and ruin! Even in this world then, can one hair of a good, noble man perish? And must it not be that this man, the friend of her soul, the arbiter of her life, who, when he quitted her, had left darkness and death to surround her, would here, in this very house, here where he had scattered the seed of so much that was good, reap the fruits of his noble deeds. No, no, Ellinor could not believe that there could be any danger for him now.

Robertson left this pleasing delusion undisturbed. He exaggerated the protection which an English house affords, and the rights of such a house. He would not trouble the sweet waking dream which she was dreaming. What then, if she were to shut her eyes, if sleep should demand its rights! She would still fancy herself in a sea of flowers, in a lake of melodies, if she mounted into her bed; and when she thought with what joy she should awake in the morning and greet the rising sun, "How could I sleep!" she exclaimed, throwing open the window and drinking in the night air.

But her father shut the window again and bade her compose herself, and pray to God for strength to bear the happiness of the morrow with discretion.

It was only when her father, concealing his anxieties, was taking a cheerful and happy leave of her, that Ellinor danced up to him and with her arms round his neck asked,

"But, my dear little Father, where are you going to sleep to-night?"

"Do not distress yourself about that. I have arranged my bed," said the old man, shutting the door of his daughter's room after him, and holding it so long that she perceived his decided wish was that she should not carry her filial anxieties any further.

All was still in the house. The god with the poppy crown reigned supreme in every corner. Though there was one who was not asleep, he held his breath and took care not to disturb the slumbers of the others. He listened anxiously whether any sound could be heard beside the watchmen's rattles in the streets and the occasional strokes of the clocks in the clocktowers. Trembling, picturing to himself what he should do if a knocking should suddenly be heard at his door, thinking what he should say, then again laughing at the fancies of his excited imagination, he gazed once more at the guest lying on his bed. The fugitive snored as though he would make up for the sleep of the seven nights he had lost. His breast heaved, the veins in his neck were swollen. His face, which had been so pallid, became flushed. His blood seemed to circulate more regularly, the action of the heart, into which fear always presses the whole current of life, appeared now to be gentle and tranquil.

Perhaps if Arthur Maxwell had on this night dreamed how his drawn sword protected a night wanderer who with a basket on his back, an iron-tipped staff, a woollen cap pulled down low over his face, issued from a low arched door and success-fully, or at least unmolested, vanished quickly in the damp fog which fills the streets of London with impenetrable darkness; if this figure which had often both sleeping and waking, risen before his memory, had appeared to him again amid the confused chaos which doubtless at this moment in his sleep shrouded the not totally lulled activity of his mind, then had he awaked and opened his eyes he might have found his dream a reality.

For, had any one been lingering at this hour at

"The Pitcher without a handle" (in our day a bright light at the entrance would announce "A night porter kept here") he might have seen a figure stealing along under the wall, rising like a shadow from the background. For from head to foot it was grey and dusky. Now, and in the present aspect of London at night, the nightly wanderer might easily be followed in a sea of pleasure and luxury. In these days, music would resound around the spy together with the bustle of carriages, and of footpassenger coming from the theatres, saloons, restaurants and oyster-houses. At the corner of every street a bag-piper would be playing some Irish air accompanying the song of an old Megæra leading a pretty, ragged child by the hand.

But a hundred and fifty years ago, the stillness of death lay at that hour over the streets of London. Nothing was to be seen but the lights in the old towers, the lanterns of the watchmen in the air against danger of fire.

All beside was black as death or despair. Even the stars, images of hope, were, like all consolations in misery, only visible to those who sought them with practised eyes. Our nocturnal wanderer is like a mole in the bosom of the earth. He knows his way. He turns right and left. Sometimes he stands still and pokes with his staff at some object which seems to have hemmed in his steps.

None but the watchmen who were stationed at the entrances of the streets noticed him. Not any of the military patrols who marched about with burning torches; all England was then in a state of siege. Not one of those who, belated, were gliding through the streets, no follower of those callings to which night belongs, looked at him. Not one of those women who hasten to and fro in hideous disguises to assist at the entrance of newcomers into this world of sorrows. Indeed, at many a house an anxious messenger was knocking and holding his lantern so as to shine on the house-sign, to convince himself that he had not mistaken the house of the able doctor whom he was breathlessly summoning to some sick bed.

"Woe! woe!" seemed to be the cry throughout all these streets. This world is a world of mourning! She is not herself aware of it when she judges by the waking hours. She must see herself when all around is slumber and sleep, fully to understand that God exercises patience and longsuffering until men have found the way, the true way in which they should walk.

And the little lamp at the wanderer's breast is

like the light of the miner in the deep shaft in the earth.

Why does he now stand still and examine something so attentively?

A paper?

He throws it behind him into the basket which he carries.

He gropes on further with his stick, the noise of which one may already hear in Covent Garden, where even at this period fruit and vegetables were sold.

Everything in the pretty arcades which surround it seemed to be alive. Here, a sleeper was stretched on the ground; there, a family were crouching on the straw collected from the market. Round the great pillar with the sun-dial in the centre of the square, the retail dealers, who wished to be first in the morning to buy the fruits coming in from the country, were huddled together.

The wanderer turned towards Drury Lane. There he began to walk more slowly. Often he stood still, sometimes he stooped down, sometimes he held something which he had picked up close to his little lamp. Most things he threw away. Now and again something was dropped over his shoulders into his basket.

The light threw its faint rays on a gate-way with

a passage for carriages and two narrow gates for foot-passengers. Two large statues looked down gloomily and gravely on the dusky streets, which were here broken at that time by gardens and detached mansions, which ran down to the Thames. Here stands Temple Bar, where the increased size of this city of the world has now caused pavement to be laid over every shoe's breadth of earth. There the gay world of London once made their promenade. There in byegone years the old Templars had dwelt, who in England, as in France, had been compelled to succumb to the jealousy and avarice of a king. Here gardens, palaces, beautiful terraces afforded an opportunity of obtaining, even from the dirty waters of the Thames, reviving air coming fresh from the sea.

Here, all is still as a churchyard, and the wanderer has nothing to feel uneasy about or to fear. Who would attack an old beggar who only looks about on the ground, and picks up the riband lost by some beauty; here, finds an artificial flower under a real one; there, pockets a shining buckle which has adorned the pretty foot of some sylph who flitted about among these encircled flowerbeds!

The city is reached. The wanderer walks more and more slowly. He passes through a gate, which was at that time still standing, on his way to the inner portion of the city of London. His road lay by the Mansion House, by the Exchange, and by St. Paul's. The fires which have so often raged in London have now given to all these buildings new fronts and a very different appearance from that which they had then. At the Exchange, the wanderer searched under all the arcades which extended right and left, a protecting cover from the rain which was beginning to drop from the ever darkening sky. But even here his inquiring eye was not at rest. Here, too, he stooped down, and his little lamp gave him light for his examination of sundry objects which lay before or behind the round archways.

Then he turned southwards. There stood the blood-stained Tower! Four towers reared themselves on high with their strange signs of vanes adorned with crowns and imperial globes. Work was still going on there by night in the royal mint. The noise of the heavily falling stamp was audible. Ah! how clear and silvery was the sound at night as the stamp of the head of King George the First fell on the round shillings! The new money with the insignia of the victory won could not be circulated quickly enough, and the glowing furnace was never allowed to grow cold at night. Perchance if the slumbers of night fled from the state criminals, then even amid the darkness they heard the triumph of the victorious thing which pleased, not Cato, but the Gods.

The clock at St. Paul's had already struck two with its strong, sonorous strokes. A Dutch chime began to sound. The wanderer fled shuddering from the precincts of the Tower and its twenty-one wards, called "Hamlets." The whole of the munitions of war in England were at that time contained within this fortress.

Our nocturnal wanderer, who had just found and secured a handsome cocked hat which had probably belonged to some intoxicated person, was on the point of entering Bishopsgate Street, when he heard the sound of horse's hoofs coming hurriedly on.

A horseman came dashing from Holborn up Canon Street.

The clatter of his sabre announced him even from a distance to be a soldier.

Doubtless he was riding to the Tower.

At the moment in which the wanderer recognised him as a dragoon of a Scotch regiment, and while the sparks from the feet of the horse (whose rider was, indeed, rushing hurriedly to the Tower) still played round the watcher upon the large stones, which were at that time used for paving, a pouch, fastened to a belt over the shoulder, fell from the horseman without his perceiving his loss.

Whether owing to the darkness or to his uncertainty as to his way in the streets, so it was that he did not observe that that portion of his equipment, which was on this occasion doubtless its most important part, had slipped from him. Probably the tongue of the buckle became loosened, or slipped in the speed of the ride.

A large, locked, courier's pouch lay before the wanderer.

He took it up. The sound of the horse's hoofs grew more and more distant in the stillness of night. Doubtless the horseman only became aware of his loss on his arrival at the Tower.

No one was near. All around was still. A stream of running water, and the noise made by the dragoon, which was now dying away in the distance, were the only sounds audible.

The pouch, which was not particularly heavy, found its way into the basket with the other things which had been preserved.

The road back — strange to say! — again to the "Flying Horse" in Cavendish Street might have taken about an hour. Yet it was not there, not beneath the sign of his house impressively eloquent in the ideas of the wanderer, but through the small back door at cross corners from the "Pitcher without a handle" that the little grey man disappeared.

Night passed away. The sun struggled through the fog. Of all those in the "Flying Horse," who had rested and dreamed and had closed the preceding day with happy hopes, Ellinor woke the earliest. She had in no way lost the thread of the inexpressible happiness which had been granted to her on the previous evening. The god of dreams had continued the weaving of the flowery chain, had twined it round her more and more closely; and when she opened her eyes, all was just as she had dreamed, just as wonderful, as incredible, as reassuring of the Eternal love, which only afflicts man in order to reward him, even in this life, with heavenly joys if he endure with patience.

The sun peeped in at the window and laughed away all scruples that the first words which crossed her lips after her morning prayer should be falsehoods.

"Miss Sarah!" she cried to the new companion, "what do you think? A cousin came to our house last night! From Canada! He is sleeping downstairs in my father's room."

By degrees all the household heard the news;

It spread upstairs and down. It travelled with the milkman to the baker, and to the butcher across the street. It was certain that a guest had arrived in the house, one long looked-for, but one who was still exhausted with his long voyage.

How Ellinor laughed, and pretended only to know her cousin a little! She might indeed know what he was like. She described him as he must have been many years before! She had known him as a little boy! He had then been like her mother's brother who was dead! His accent was rather Scotch, for the Wilsons had formerly lived in Scotland. And amidst all these inventions, she ordered breakfast to be laid in the state room on the middle floor, sent for the best butter that could be procured, had the whitest loaf cut and made into toast, and even cut a large new York ham and ordered up some dried Tay salmon; for this river abounds in salmon.

It is true that Ellinor hesitated a little at the inquiries of the servants, and at those of Miss Sarah, a rather laboriously preserved beauty of incalculable age who was formally preparing herself to fall in love; all of which inquiries tended to the point where Mr. John Robertson himself had slept that night. Her only anxiety was lest her father should have taken cold by sleeping on one of the many couches downstairs. But she was well aware that the lower part of the house, so little accessible even to her, had within it many more comforts than the servants of the house knew of. There were cloaks and wraps enough there and, indeed, her mother's old bed was down below and still almost close at hand.

That she need not expect her father until probably eleven o'clock, was certain. She did not know how she should act if Lord Arthur should make his appearance earlier. However, she believed that she might be at ease, that Lord Arthur knew the customs of the house from long, and what had been to her happy experience, and had learnt to accomodate himself to them.

Yet, perhaps, it might be that her lover would come up from her father's room before the latter. Perhaps, that she might then be induced to take this early meal alone with him. She relied on her power to play her part with successful dissimulation. Then she danced up and downstairs singing, and thought to herself that Arthur would hear her voice and would no longer be able to withstand his yearning to greet her. If for a time she paused in her loud warblings, which resounded throughout the house, it was because she said to herself, "But how is it, are you still mistress of your modicum of brains? Have you not dreamt it all? Did your father really come to your door yesterday evening, and sit on your bed and tell you this wonderful news? Or suppose the whole thing has been a jest of your father's?"

But she knew him too well for that, knew that fancies of that kind were foreign to his nature.

Just as Ellinor had finished adorning herself as much as was allowable for a person in mourning, and had put on diamond earrings, which sparkled like dewdrops on the round rolls of her fair hair (Miss Sarah had introduced quite new fashions to those of Miss Kitty), a messenger came up from her father to tell her to hasten down to him immediately.

Suspecting nothing wrong, she threw every thing on her toilette glass aside; did not take the precaution of making a last criticism on her charming appearance in the mirror, but danced like a child (she was near taking two steps at a time) down to her father's closed apartments.

There a strange sight awaited her. Lord Arthur was there, certainly. But no shaggy beard disguised him, as she had supposed. This had already fallen beneath her father's shaving apparatus. Indeed her lover stood before her in an elegant dress (though assuredly in rather a contracted one, since the clothes belonged to her father), in red silk and like a sea lobster on his own account, only in different form, slight in figure as ever, but rather pale, and at this moment also perceptibly moved, yet more by joy than by fear, although the latter was not wanting.

Fear was, on the contrary, openly expressed in the face of her father who had immediately locked the door again softly; and the emotional embrace, which served to the lovers instead of words, was hidden from the inquisitive eyes of the other occupants of the house, as the words which followed were from their ears.

But what did her father look like? He wore a laced uniform, a gay-coloured girdle round his waist, shoes, bright, flaming stockings, shoulderknots on his shoulders, he was the personification of a lacquey from the aristocratic quarter of Pall Mall. And yet there was no room for laughter. In her father's face there was the accustomed look of sunshine, and yet he stood as though transfixed. The light in it was like that of the winter sun shining on ice. His thoughts seemed to be present, not so his eyes. His silence, his movement as he pushed the happy pair back into the inner room not exposed to eavesdroppers, had in them something which stood in strong antagonism with Ellinor's expectations.

"My all!" cried Lord Arthur, throwing his arm

impetuously round the fair form of his faithful love. "Come now what will! Death itself has no terrors for me now that I have seen this moment, been reunited to my poor, unhappy Ellinor!"

"Oh! no, not unhappy!" Ellinor would have said. But the words died on her lips, as she looked at her father.

Lord Arthur also turned towards him.

"Calm yourself, Father John," said he, embracing the old man. "If your labours for my deliverance should not succeed, and if your noble, unmerited sacrifice for the preservation of my life should prove vain, you may still say that you have given a man a foretaste of heaven during his last hours upon earth—"

Ellinor stood speechless and began to tremble.

"Yes! that a man could exist," burst forth Lord Arthur with passion, extending his clenched fist towards Heaven, as though asseverating before God, as though in an act of vindication, "a man who could use his last moment of life in the service of the devil—"

"Oh! what is the matter?" exclaimed Ellinor, uttering a cry. Her heart could no longer control itself. It threatened to break. "You speak of him! What did he do to you?"

She thought of Sam and stood trembling, waiting for an answer. She felt indeed that the dreams of happiness, of security, of undisturbed intercourse with the man whom she had learnt to receive and to acknowledge as the object of her affections had passed all too quickly. Either the position of her beloved friend had not at first been so favourable as Ellinor had supposed yesterday from the auspicious words of her father, or else it had changed for the worse from some newly arisen circumstances.

The manner, the dress of her father were to her so astonishing that she could hardly understand them. Whilst Lord Arthur drew her unceasingly to his side, showered kisses upon her and called her father not only his saviour but a priest, a saint, who now so generously and nobly permitted the long pent up feelings of his children (he called himself his son) to have full vent, the father himself was occupied, almost indeed like a servant, in packing some trunks which lay round about, half filled and still unlocked. The doors of the cupboard stood open. The father put some heavy bags of gold, which it required some exertion to lift, into the trunks and covered the bags with clothes. He told Ellinor, on her part, to collect quickly her best clothes, her most costly trinkets and all that she had that was valuable and to put them into a large chest which was in one of the store-rooms at the top of the house, well-known and accessible to her.

"We must take a journey to Scotland immediately, my child," he said, as tears of sad foreboding arose to Ellinor's eyes; "and keep up the cheerful look," continued he anxiously, "which has hitherto been on your countenance. Let it appear to all in the house that it is a pleasant journey which you are going to take with me. The reason why I have dressed myself like a servant, and why we are to start immediately, you shall learn while we are on our way. I will now throw a cloak over my dress that I may not betray myself to anybody. Provide some breakfast down here, but not until you are certain that no one can see my dress. Send Toby to the posthouse and order a postilion and four horses to come immediately, and send also to Mr. Twistle to let me have the best and strongest of his carriages, the blue one you understand, that with the gold ornamentation, and say that it is for a long journey. Provide everything, my darling, and remember that a man must earn his happiness. Ha! ha! this will be a splendid journey, we three together. Laugh! laugh! away over the autumn fields under the shade of the red mountain ash, merrily, merrily, forward we go! And now bring us something to eat, do you hear?"

Ellinor hastened, amid smiles and tears, to obey her father's orders. Lord Arthur pressed her once more impulsively to his heart and said,

"We must fly, Ellinor. No," he added interrupting himself, "it is I alone who must fly, but the immeasurable goodness of your father, of our father, would lead him to share with me the fearful danger which awaits me."

"What danger?" cried Ellinor.

"Pooh, pooh, danger!" said her father interrupting her and his friend, and pushing Ellinor out of the room with his right hand, while with his left he thrust a large bag of gold into his breast. "We may laugh at all the crown-constables and at the Lord Chief Justice into the bargain."

Ellinor did not know what influence it was which gave her strength to carry out everything which her father had required of her. Was it the spirit of childlike obedience? Was it the exciting example which in great difficulties lends us strength such as we should never have imagined ourselves capable of? Or was it love which shed its powerful influence for the first time over the soul of the young girl; which proved to her for the first time how it raises man above himself and makes his spirit fly boldly aloft? That it was probably the despair which Ellinor experienced in losing again immediately the wonderful good she had just gained, this she did not confess to herself.

Everything was arranged by her as her father had desired. The servants, the cook, Toby who was sent off post-haste to the post-house and to Mr. Twistle, all these were not a little astonished when they heard that the cousin who had arrived from the colonies was obliged to go immediately to Scotland to claim an inheritance. They ran hither and thither and helped to pack. Nor were they less astonished when Mr. Robertson himself appeared in a large red travelling-cloak which closely enveloped the whole of his little person, breakfasted hurriedly with his nephew, and ordered the heavy boxes in the meantime to be carried into the hall, that they might be ready to be lifted immediately and in the shortest possible time into the carriage which was expected. The cousin from Canada too eat, laughed, packed, passed his hand thoughtfully over his forehead, all by turns. Certainly he was a surprisingly handsome young man, this backwoodsman from America, who cut short all questions, inquiries, astonishment and shakings of the head with no further trouble than the impression made by his handsome person.

"I do not know how long I shall remain absent," said John Robertson to his head servant whilst he was making his arrangements; "the business which calls us away requires our presence in different towns and in different ways. Perhaps everything may be arranged in England; if our affairs are finished in Broxbourne, I shall return in two days; if we are obliged to go to Buntingford, then we shall be away four days. But if there are any difficulties respecting the property which can only be arranged in the Scotch courts, then it will be fourteen days. Take care then of the "Flying Horse" for me; be honest and true; the longer I remain away, the larger will be the present that we shall bring back."

The new companion Miss Sarah had the wonderful thought to say to the inhabitants of the basement floor that they might have noticed that Mr. Robertson had sometimes said, "we come back" and sometimes only "I come back." "Suppose this return of the cousin from Canada had something significant in it," she said. "Perhaps a bridegroom, who, on account of Mr. Sam" (here all her listeners shuddered with horror and only nodded in token of agreement), "had not been able to declare himself openly but had not permitted himself to marry. Many marriages," she said, "were arranged in this way quite quietly and only first became public when"—Miss Sarah reserved the narration of those instances which had fallen under her own experience for the golden time of her sole reign in the house. Now it was necessary to bustle about and help the travellers, whose haste was repeatedly retarded by calculations of the peculiar circumstances with which questions of inheritance are wont to be combined in this imperfect world.

The journey was not begun until some hours after midday. All Cavendish Street was astonished at the brilliant carriage which stood before the house, the "Flying Horse." "Has the old man been made a baronet?" they asked. "Is he tormented with pride since his son-in-law was elevated to such high honours?" And, as usual, remarks were plentiful among those who stood around the carriage which was laden with boxes and trunks. The strangest thing of all, that so luxurious a journey should be taken without the attendance of a servant, was only noticed after the travellers had gone away. Up to that moment, all hands in the house who were available had helped in packing the carriage and provisions for the journey.

Now London streets, together with the rattling of a four-horse-carriage over the embankments of rubbish which at that time were called pavement, are not places where one can explain strange and mysterious things, not even when in a carriage. Nor was this needed by Ellinor. She knew indeed why Lord Arthur Maxwell had leaned back in one corner of the carriage, why, by holding up his cloak, he had avoided the inquisitive glances which were cast into the carriage. The carriages of those days were indeed cumbrously large and wide, but they bore a similarity with the light carriages of doctors and speculators of our day in this, that the step by which they were entered was raised scarcely a hand's breadth from the ground.

"Yes! Ellinor understood all now, even the sudden happiness which had come to her as from heaven. Three things only she could not understand. First, why Arthur should not have been safe in their quiet house which was so little troubled by visitors; secondly, why the journey was to be made to Scotland, where the very supreme court was sitting from which their dear friend was seeking to escape; and thirdly, what the strange servant's dress of her father meant.

On this last point she became enlightened. And also on the other two.

The carriage had scarcely reached Hackney (a village which, as regards its original aspect, has quite disappeared, and is now absorbed into the town) when her father told the postilion to stop.

"Where does this road lead?" he cried to the postilion, through a window which opened from the inside direct upon the saddle horse.

"To Barnet, Sir," was the answer.

"To Barnet? Are you then mad?" cried Ellinor's father to her great astonishment. "Who wants to go to Barnet or indeed to Hertfordshire at all?"

"But that is the road to Scotland, Sir."

"Who wants to go to that hot country! Scotland! Who do you think wants in these days to go to Scotland?"

"But," replied the postilion turning round in perplexity, "the postmaster said—"

"The postmaster said what he at first knew," answered Robertson. "My master has been obliged to change his plan, since be received an express before he started, summoning him across the bridge to Woolwich. Where were your ears when I told you on entering the carriage—"

"You did not speak a word to me, Sir," the postilion began to explain, and became rude.

"Do not call me, 'Sir,'" replied Robertson in a determined tone; "I am a servant as well as you, and am only sitting in the carriage with my lord and my lady to attend to the expenses. You will soon see that I shall mount the box, and then I will teach you to make stupid jokes. Good Heavens! the sun is already setting. Now turn round and show all London your brightly polished boots once more; that in truth is what you wanted."

Ellinor bit her lips for laughing and sat full of

expectation and anxious about what might happen. The sly look in her father's eyes, the joyful satisfaction on Arthur's features showed her that there was some mutual understanding between them. At home people had been made to believe that they were going to travel to Scotland, whilst, in truth, they were seeking the only safe place, the nearest sea-coast, the Port of Dover. From there the flight of the man she loved to France would be feasible. This prospect was certainly sad enough. But thoughts of separation could not find much place in a heart which was still filled with joy in the happiness of reunion.

The noise of the town once more prevented any further conversation; the grand four-horse coach was turned round and was conducted back by the postilion, who had been flattered into good humour by the praise of his boots, through the same streets through which it had rolled before; who wondered at it amid the bustle of a beautiful autumn day in London, where multitudes were moving up and down, and one crowd was replaced by another? Here, such an object was but as a drop in the ocean. London Bridge was reached. The fog from the Thames was already mixing with the evening twilight. Towards the East, the towers and windows of the Tower were already lighted up by the rays of the setting sun. On the right, the clouds and fog extended like a military escort accompanying the departing king of day on his disappearance in the sea. Violet, dark blue, yellow, purple, more beautiful than the colours of a ray of light caught in a prism were the hues of the clouds which surrounded the sun as it journeyed on like a ball of fire, and which hung like golden fringe over the large, old, grey palaces that skirted the winding banks of Thames, and lay like purple cushions on a forest of masts and spread their canopies over the asylums for the sick and superannuated, over the hospitals and refuges for invalids. One could no longer distinguish what was still immoveable, what dissolving, what lasting splendour, what the phantasmagoria of the moment.

The carriage rolled through the south suburb of the city, and night had already set in when it arrived in Woolwich, that arsenal of the English navy, that gigantic quay for her ships which were already becoming more adventurous and more and more capable of defying the anger of Neptune.

Here began a long negociation with the postilion, a debate which was carried on in the most persuasive manner and with a handsome present by the servant of Lord and Lady Derville (as Mr. Robertson, now throwing off his cloak and thus proclaiming his humble position and the appropriateness of the seat outside) called his master and his master's wife. The light shed into the interior of the carriage by the lanterns of the custom-house officers and naval officials displayed to view two young beings who seemed to have been made for each other, handsomely dressed according to the prevailing fashion of the gay youth of the day, yet so strikingly modest, indeed more than modest, perhaps embarrassed, at being disturbed in what was certainly a very happy tête-à-tête.

Ellinor's opposition to the manner, scarcely prudent even for a young person, in which her father had mounted on the front seat of the carriage, and had insisted on remaining all night on the box, was restrained by Arthur who whispered to her, "My dearest, this noble sacrifice of your father's in wishing to play the part of our servant was already early this morning the subject of a discussion between us which I was obliged to promise him should not be repeated. I entreated him that through every gate through which we must pass, and that whenever we should be questioned by Walpole's numerous emissaries, the answers should run thus, "It is old Lord Derville who is travelling to Paris with his daughter, attended by a young servant newly engaged, whom I wished to represent. However, he insisted that an old servant of the house of Derville should have the pleasure and, at the same time, the honour of taking the wedding-journey, which was to be devoid of all splendour, with his young master to Paris."

It was indeed a foretaste of future bliss to Ellinor, this traversing in dark night the silent, solemn woods of Kent, passing over the waving, undulating hills which form the bulwarks of London towards the sea, pressed to the heart of her lover who spread his cloak around them both and cherished and soothed her as a mother her child; and all this, under the protection and in compliance with the wishes of an affectionate father.

"The wedding-tour," thought Ellinor, "that is certainly a joke (the darkness hid her blushes at the idea) such as takes place in comedies where three people have the courage to enter into a conflict with the tricks of fortune."

Their road lay by Dartford, Rochester and Canterbury to Dover. This was, at that time, the shortest way to France, but also the most dangerous. The nearer they drew to the coast, the more numerous and frequent were the roving patrols which the travellers met. Often enough, Lord Derville was driven into straits by captious inquiries. Most of the questions were answered, however, by his old servant with expressions of unwillingness that the happiness of the lovers should be disturbed. The beautiful chalk cliffs which adorn the sea-coast of England were reached on the following evening and at the time of a gorgeous sun-set. On the way it had become apparent that Lord Arthur was encircled by some mystery. He saw clearly what danger surrounded him and how generously intent John Robertson was on saving him from death by a cannon shot or by the sword of the xecutioner. But one thing he could not understand, and he asked Ellinor with expressions of the liveliest wonder, how her father could have known with such certainty of the destruction which awaited him. Her father had represented his life to him as hanging on a hair and his danger as being imminent owing to the very refuge he had sought in Robertson's house. The whole depths of Samuel Mordaunt's nature were now opened to Ellinor's view, the abyss into which she might have been destined to enter for the whole period of her life, and in the same proportion have been plunged into incalculable woe. Was she right to assent to the suppositions of Lord Arthur, who would have opposed such unheard of wickedness in the heart of a former friend, so valued by him, and so attractive in many ways? Lord Arthur only said,

"It was the fear of death which induced him, when before the judges, to commit this disgraceful act of treachery. They must have tortured him to the utmost to make him give up the names of those with whom he was implicated. The first inquiry must have been respecting my position which belonged to the nobility of Scotland and involved military duties. To order me to be shot was more welcome to the court-martial than to order a lawyer to be hung. And yet Sam was obliged to part with life! Sam, who clung to this life with all the fibres of a soul which his creed did not hold to be immortal! Sam, who carried about with him a whole world of plans for the future and dreamed of the most glowing consummations! Sam, who could call an Ellinor, you my beloved one, his own!"

"Oh!" said Ellinor turning away, and she looked out on the autumnal-tinted country which was bounded by the lofty, distant towers of the great cathedral at Canterbury. She was of so gentle a disposition that she could not even at this moment speak of the acquaintance which she had gradually made with the existence of the Viscountess de Champfleury, who had arrived safely in France, the object of Sam's last thought.

Sam, in order to save himself from death, had given information about his fellow-conspirators. He had described the place in Fish Lane Corner where the French lady had, at the house of a fellow countryman (a disguised priest who had purchased a practice as dentist), laid the detailed plans of the Pretender before the boldest of the young nobles, the successors of the old cavaliers of Cromwell's time, and had bound them by a solemn oath which Sam, who had by accident mixed with the conspirators, had been obliged to take together with them and had willingly taken. Young Derwentwater's threat to stab him if he did not join with them in everything was not needed at that time. The charming appearance of the Frenchwoman in her disguise as a man, her flattering words, the marks of preference which she bestowed on him, had at once overcome all other feelings. But now, Sam had betrayed the houses, the families, where the fugitives should be sought. Only through his treachery, owing to fear of death, was it possible that such a paper should exist as that which Arthur drew from his breast-pocket and gave to Ellinor to read. . It ran thus,

"Head Quarters, Haslingden, 20th October, 1715.
To the Lord Governor of the Tower, in the King's name.

As the Lieutenant in expectance, Lord Arthur Maxwell, taken in open warfare against the troops of the Crown to which he swore allegiance, and with weapons in his hand, has been sentenced to be shot by judgment of a court-martial, but has found an opportunity to gain his freedom by escaping from his escort, has wandered about in different parts of the Kingdom and doubtless at this moment is in London: And as in consequence of the deposition of the traitor, Samuel Mordaunt, executed on Bleasdale Moor and formerly a lawyer, concerning the origin and progress of the rebellion, which with God's help is now put down, it may be assumed that the aforesaid condemned Lord Arthur Maxwell has taken refuge in a house in Cavendish Street called the "Flying Horse" and inhabited by one John Robertson: Your Lordship will immediately arrest him at the aforesaid place, if he be to be found there, and order the sentence of the court-martial to be carried out within twenty-four hours after his arrest.

Signed, Col. Hutchinson,
President of His Majesty's Court-martial
in Lancashire."

"How did this fearful paper come into your hands?" asked Ellinor, who had grown paler and paler at every line she read.

"That is what I ask your father," answered Lord Arthur; "I owe it to him that this death-warrant has not reached the Governor of the Tower."

Ellinor covered her face with her hands. She felt that the answer, which her lover had given her, corroborated the reports which were set abroad about her father.

"How did it happen before," continued Lord Arthur, "that John Robertson handed over the lost note-book to the traitor? For indeed, you heard afterwards why on that occasion, when the unhappy man met us walking by moonlight in your little garden, he seemed to have lost all self-control, embraced you, and appeared to think the possession of your love worth all else in the world."

Ellinor was again unable to answer a word. Confusion at her own silence overpowered her to such a degree, that she still kept her eyes covered with both hands and now, indeed also, that the tears which filled them might not be seen.

Lord Arthur saw the painful effect of his questions and restrained the utterance of his astonishment, only to save Ellinor. He forbore to speak of his wonder at the manner in which Robertson seemed to live. But he carried out the intention which he had at first entertained, of asking Ellinor about the nocturnal wanderer, whom he had seen gliding forth from their house like a ghost. Yet his slightest hints on the subject caused Ellinor such pain, that it seemed as though she must break open the carriage windows to get air to breathe.

It was impossible in accordance with the part which Robertson had taken and which he played with wonderful self-devotion, that the three persons so closely united should in any way consult together upon their next measures while on their journey.

His conviction that a young pair of lovers (as they were said to be), travelling to France, must prefer to remain undisturbed was maintained by the old servant with a varied loquacity, which was often quite comic, to all who would have made inquiries in the interior of the carriage. Any prolonged time for the two or three to stand together could only take place when the horses were changed, and it was incumbent then to keep up the characters which the travelling party had assumed. This must be done, above all, at the inn at Dover, the "Crown," where almost all the negociators for the transit to Calais (plenty of whom offered themselves immediately after the arrival of the travellers at this smallest but liveliest of the seven harbours of England) were under the control of an armed coast-guard or harbour-police. Embrasures mounted with cannon commanded the little town on all sides from the castle on the rock, which was now lighted up by the setting sun with a magic glow. From it, any suspected vessel might easily be greeted in a most unwelcome manner.

The regular mail-packet was the only conveyance that could be selected for the passage, for this vessel alone would sail early on the following morning. Other vessels gave promises of speedy departure, which were by no means to be relied on. But even this mail-packet was under the strictest control. Not only was it surrounded by soldiers and constables during the time for embarkation, but a sufficient number also remained on the deck and kept their eyes upon the passengers during the voyage. Lists of the proscribed might be read at all the entrances. In these, all magistrates were required, each according to his ability, to render the escape of the conspirators impossible. Rewards were offered, which might induce so speculative a people as the English to support the police. Lord Arthur Maxwell stood named among those whose capture and delivery was most urgently recommended to all magistrates. By the number of messengers on horseback, the orderlies, the couriers, whom the travellers had already met on their way, they had perceived the vigour with which the prescribed measures were carried out.

They partook of supper in the best room in the "Crown." Robertson assisted in waiting. Ellinor began to be sorrowful; she thought that the hour for parting was come. The negociations at the mail-packet office her father had undertaken alone.

But how astonished was she, when the old man, just before they retired for the night, said to her and Lord Arthur, "My children, there is no help for it; we must even now say our farewells. To-morrow we shall be watched at every step, therefore let us part now."

With these words, he extended his left hand to Lord Arthur, his right he would have given to Ellinor. His daughter drew back in alarm and exclaimed,

"Father, you do not mean to take leave of me too? How am I to understand you? If we are going to France, surely you are coming with us."

With a melancholy smile, Robertson shook his venerable head.

"Dearest Sir," said Arthur amazed, "what is your intention?"

"If you were to cross quite alone, my son," began Robertson calmly and endeavouring to conceal the tremulousness of his voice and the tears which would spring to his eyes, "you would be an object of universal curiosity. The announcement to which we have adhered from London till now, that you were a newly married pair, starting on your journey to France, without passports and without any thought of the possibility of being questioned and searched, would then be involved in serious perplexities. On the contrary, if Ellinor remains with you and you are solely occupied with her on board the vessel, with no thought but for finding shelter for her, and of supporting her if she should be unwell, and taking care that she wants for nothing: then no one will trouble himself about you, nor examine your features, nor compare them with the descriptions which I have already seen placed in the hands of the inspectors. On the deck of the vessel I shall take leave of you, and in such a manner as becomes an old servant. Promise me then, my Lord Arthur, and you, my child, promise not to make a scene; and then," and the old man raised his voice in solemn tones, "then, my Lord, promise me further, that in France you will enter the first church of our faith (in Calais you will find one such, although without tower and without bells, which symbols an heretical temple for prayer is not allowed to raise in France) and there take mutual vows as man and wife, honourably united and bound together."

The two young people stood at first as though

stunned. Then, with mixed feelings of happiness and anguish, they fell together on the old man's breast.

"In the chests," continued Robertson, "you will find sufficient to live comfortably in a strange land and to enable you to write to your father that you are happy, and to console him with the hope that the hour will not fail to come in which the wrath of the reigning sovereign shall be allayed, and a public amnesty including yourself also shall enable you to tread once more the loved soil of your fatherland."

"But why do not you yourself go with us?" asked Arthur, with feelings of pain at the approaching parting; "remain with us, conduct us to the altar, be our witness, our counseller. We will go thither even as your servants."

"Yes, father," added Ellinor, "how can I live without you?"

Robertson looked cautiously around, as though the walls might become traitors. Then with a grave earnestness and his whole bearing showing the firmness of his resolve, he said,

"No, I must return."

"But you may yourself lose your liberty," replied Lord Arthur, and Ellinor cried so bitterly on hearing this and lamented so much the idea of such a possibility, that her father said to her in an earnest tone,

"We shall all be betrayed if you do not control yourself."

At this, Lord Arthur lowered his voice, whilst he continued,

"If that which was frustrated by an accident, if that which God himself must have sent to you (for in no other way can I interpret it) should be recovered, if people should enter your house and should learn that I have been there and that I have saved myself by a flight to France—"

"Get over there first," interrupted Robertson quickly, "all the rest is my affair."

Ellinor understood that her father could not bear to part from his house and property. Let him take with him as much as he would, it was certain that he must still leave half his fortune behind. She stood weeping and would have given utterance to the confession that she could not part from her father, whom she had to cherish and to care for in his old age. But Robertson cut short the confession which he foresaw was coming. He perceived whence the sudden irresolution of his child proceeded and said,

"You alone can save Lord Arthur. His young

wife alone can do this. Men as a rule rejoice with those whom the rare opportunities of life permit them to call truly happy and whom they can look upon with pleasure. In your happiness, in your laughing and talking, in your gentle chattering and whispering, each one will see a type of his own better days or of the time which he wishes may one day break upon himself. Give me your word of honour, my lord, that you will be married in Calais. By the power of that office which God gives to every one who is baptized into his name, by that priestly influence of love and faith which dwells in the heart of every Christian, I place your hands in each other and bless you as a Christian husband and wife before God and say thereto, Amen."

Ellinor knelt down, Lord Maxwell followed her example. Her father laid his hands on their heads and blessed them.

"The wife is the glory of her husband," said he, "a diligent wife is his crown, but she must be subject to him; her ornament, her true ornament is the favour she finds in the eyes of her husband and of God."

The pair thus bound together by the invisible Church were so overcome, so filled with emotion by the contemplation of the consequences which must ensue from their father's blessing, that John Robertson had withdrawn before they perceived it. The publicity of an inn rendered the continuation of an explanation impossible.

On the following morning, the regular packet took this pair, united before God, on board. Robertson superintended the embarkation and the putting on board of the luggage, and smoothed every difficulty which might have arisen from inquiries and a more minute examination of Lord and Lady Derville. He added yet one more effort of paternal sternness to the great anguish of his heart. He reminded Ellinor (who at the moment of parting threatened to break down) with one of those sharp glances which could sometimes flash from his usually mild and childlike eyes, that she must remember the demeanour which became her at this moment and which would be in accordance with the arrangement agreed upon. Arthur's firmness and her perception of the importance of this moment effected the rest.

Robertson once again mounted the bare, rocky heights which surround the harbour of Dover, and waved his tear-bedewed handkerchief towards the vessel which was sailing from him until this emblem of the hearts still yearning towards him had disappeared in the thick fog, which was the precursor of a fine autumn day dawning over the calm waters.

Then he returned to the "Crown," paid the bill, ordered now two, instead of four horses to Mr. Twistle's blue coach and drove back to London.

CHAPTER X.

The Judge's Sentence.

THE gloomy clouds of fate, whose approach Maxwell had foreseen for his noble preserver, certainly burst upon him very quickly. The saddest trials were awaiting him in London; such indeed as must necessarily accelarate his death.

The state of siege which existed in Great Britain, the continued sway of martial law, had caused the suspension for a considerable time of that precious liberty which King George had of necessity sworn to preserve intact, liberty in one's house under the Habeas Corpus Act. King George brought with him none of those peculiar advantages which, in later days, have adorned German princes when they have become domesticated among foreign nations as consorts of reigning sovereigns. He neither possessed learning nor any superiority of soul. He did not even know how to express himself in the idiom of the country which made advances to him with such generous self-sacrifice and with such complete and heroic sacrifice of its own flesh and blood in the suppression of the Stuart dynasty. The preference which he showed for art sprang in him from a love of splendour.

The peculiarities of a Hanoverian youth, with whom nothing transcends the pleasures of life, these displayed themselves in him, from the beginning, in following English customs, in hunting, drinking, and in undue bondage to the fair sex. These were the cement, the closest bonds, which united George with the English nobility. Whilst, as is well known, he had shut up his wife in Celle on account of her pretended unfaithfulness, he himself led two ladies of the Hanoverian nobility up the ladder to the splendid eminence which had been bestowed on his house, and presented them to the ladies of England among whom were models of the noblest womanhood, the one as Duchess of Kendal, the other as Countess of Darlington. In every other respect he allowed his minister, Robert Walpole, to rule, and this latter carried on the suppression of the rising in favour of the Stuarts with merciless severity. Thus the Earl of Kenmure, also, was beheaded in the Tower on the 24th of February 1716.

John Robertson was thrown into prison, on account of the shelter which he had given to a man convicted of high treason. In the search made in his house, strange things came to light, and among them the leathern courier's pouch which had been cut open by force. It bore the royal stamp. The discovery was soon made that it had belonged to that very dragoon who had, some time before, been sent by night with a message to the Tower which he had never been able to deliver. The unhappy soldier had been made to do penance for his offence by one of those severe punishments which were at that time, commonly inflicted in the military profession, and which still exist in the English army.

Fourteen days might have passed between the time when the notice from the Governor of the Tower had gone to Colonel Hutchinson in Lancashire and the arrival of the newly prepared dispatch. Robertson counted every day and hour till it arrived. He had done nothing to secure his own safety. He rejoiced to hear of the fate of his children, who had been united in Calais, with the blessing of the church, by the hand of a protestant naval chaplain and who had reached Paris in safety. For the rest, a dull resignation had come over him, to which the exhaustion caused by those prodigious exertions of both mind and body, which must have been demanded of a man so recently chased hither and thither, might have contributed.

When Robertson was imprisoned, full utterance was given to all the reports which had been spread regarding his origin, the manner in which he had obtained his fortune, his relations with the deceased old Mordaunt, his nocturnal journeys, the noises made in the outbuildings and his intercourse with the strange apparitions which were seen nightly to enter his house. Many of these reports, such as that John Robertson must be a smuggler or a coiner of false money, made the judges of King's Bench, whither the unfortunate man had been first taken, laugh heartily beneath their long wigs which hung down over the breast like a lion's mane. But it was not to be denied that a room full of the strangest old articles of every kind had been found in his outbuilding, nor that John Robertson looked frightened and depressed and, indeed, like a convicted criminal. The gravest discovery of all was that at his house, amongst all this rubbish, was found the pouch with the royal arms. It was the same which had been lost by the young dragoon. Had it been stolen from him? How had the prisoner come by it?

In the course of the prosecution it appeared that it was just this last article which was the special cause of Robertson's confession of a deep conviction of guilt which oppressed him. The lot of the poor soldier who had been so severely punished grieved him. He might have destroyed the leather pouch. That he had not done so was due to that inner law by which he had already judged himself before his own conscience and before God, even ere he had fallen into the hands of earthly justice. For it became more and more apparent that his strange actions were combined with a lofty and honourable mind, which had guided him through many years with conscientious strictness; a feeling of honour to which he had heen untrue for the first time, he corrected himself and said for the second time, when he found Lord Arthur Maxwell's death-warrant.

As a London citizen John Robertson, could not be tried by the ordinary judges. The Lord Mayor's court, a privilege of the City, had demanded him from the King's Bench and had summoned him before its bar, where a regular jury tried him and he was defended by one of the cleverest barristers. At that period, the mediæval custom of sanctuary prevailed in London. In any acknowledged refuge to which a man had fled or betaken himself voluntarily with consent of the law, he could await, with a certain amount of freedom, though under surveillance, the result of the prosecution.

The concourse on the day of public trial was unusually large. Robertson recognized many well-known faces among the audience. He nodded to the sexton of St. Paul's, when the latter seemed to greet him with his eyes. It seemed as though he would say, "Yes, old friend Wetherby, you will soon have me in your dominious and put my number among the rest in your books." He was only delighted that the little publicity which newspapers at that time enjoyed and the fact that most events died away within their own immediate circle had prevented the recall of his child from Paris. His resolve not to give her intelligence of his position until after the sentence should have been passed appeared, fortunately, not likely to be thwarted by any officiousness of strangers.

The arraignment of the Crown solicitor rested mainly on charges of robbery, fraud, high-treason and dishonourable occupation. The speech of the barrister who replied, fell far short of Robertson's own defence. He was not able altogether to banish the image of a miser, who slunk through the streets at night and made use for himself of things which had been inadvertently lost in the bustle of a city (which already at that time numbered a population of more than half a million) or in the throng of traffic. He had, however, as a lawyer, proved by evidence that any one who finds thing is only bound, up to a certain point, to restore it again. John Robertson had hitherto always done this honourably. His friendship with old Mordaunt had assisted him in one of the strangest occupations in the world. Through him, and by the aid of his servant Bob Wilkie, the articles which were found were always returned to their lawful owners when these could be discovered. In other cases, they had been left at Bow Street in the charge of the officer at the head of the watchmen. That this courier's pouch had been cut by the finder could, in the judgment of the counsel for the defence, only be held excusable because in this manner alone could its destination and its real owner be discovered. He who found anything was in a certain degree lord of his treasure-trove. The Roman law also granted him a portion of its value; another portion, certain laws assigned to the owner of the ground and soil whereon anything had been found. That the accused had avoided delivering a warrant of death issued against his son-in-law was an offence for which he deserved all honour. For, and here the advocate raised his voice, the English people did not share in the furious greed for revenge of the present conquerors. The change in public opinion, which had already long been making its way, came in aid of the barrister. He could venture to represent his client as a martyr to the military and aristocratic party and to the wishes of the courtiers. The reply of the solicitor, who wished throughout to maintain the accusation of robbery and high-treason, was lost and indeed completely silenced, when John Robertson himself began to speak and totally destroyed the picture which had been drawn of an avaricious miser raking for treasures in the mud of the streets.

With touching simplicity, he related the same story of his visit to the theatre in Drury Lane which he had already, more than a year ago, told to his daughter. Unassuming in his recital, which was therefore deeply touching to all hearers and even to the judge himself, he described his despair when the deed of gift, on the strength of which he had married, had been lost. Every one, full of compassion and deeply moved, could see him wandering hither and thither among the arcades of Covent Garden, Drury Lane, and the Strand, after the rolling of carriages had ceased and silence had fallen on the haunts of pleasure and dissipation; could see the despair on his features and hear the inquiries he made of passers-by. He had drawn bills of exchange on this inheritance, the time for a speedy entering upon which appeared to him so certain. He had liabilities of another kind to meet, had hired a house of business and a comfortable dwelling. For his young wife had claims to a life of easy competence and free enjoyment.

"When," continued he, in a trembling voice and after having been first invited by the president of the court to rest himself, to sit down, to revive himself with a draught of fresh water, "when," he repeated, declining the offer by a shake of his head, "when immediately after the discovery of my loss I hastened back to Drury Lane, they allowed me to seek in the now darkened theatre for what I had lost. They brought lights to all the stairs and accompanied me to the place where I had sat with my wife. Nothing was to be found. They then became impatient at the delay which I caused to the doorkeepers, showed me out of the building and locked it up. But I did not leave it altogether; I wandered round about it on all sides. Here, lay one object which attracted my attention; there, another. Formerly I should have passed these by, should have directed my looks, if not to the stars, still straight before me as one must do in London. Now I picked up everything which was to be seen on the ground. On the very first day, I found a sealed letter, a valuable earring, an eyeglass set in gold, and brought all home with me, compassionating indeed the lot of the losers but despairing bitterly, because I could not compare it in any way with my own. The journey for the purpose of shewing ourselves as the heirs was obliged to be given up. The lawyers convinced me that every hope was vain unless the deed could be produced. I sought for it anew; I sought by day-light; was present at a new performance in the theatre; it was a concert. The heavenly tones around me pierced my heart but I could not follow them. My presence in the brilliantly lighted house was only that I might renew my search within it and around it. Again I found things, but not that which had formerly been the breath of my life, the warranty of my honour. There was a ring perhaps drawn off the finger with the glove. A valuable shoe-buckle in enamel sparkled opposite to me; written papers were also among the many worthless articles which I had found. There were papers which might have been of value to someone else; estimates for the building of a large house. This was repeated for many days, for many nights, until Friday came, the day on which the weekly papers appearing on Saturday, received their last advertisements. I had already been to their offices and had promised to the finder of my deed a sum which was considerable for my means. On Friday I doubled the sum, although my forebodings as to the future began to be of the saddest. At these offices I found notices of lost articles. Before I had clearly read them I obtained pen and paper in order to advertise my loss anew. It was only when I was going away, sighing deeply, that I once more looked at the notices at hand, and perceived that it was I who had found most of the articles, the letter, the ring, the enamelled shoe-buckle. On the following day, I read in the papers that search was also being made for the earring and the eye-glass set in gold. I myself was thoroughly shaken and wearied by my night-watches. I sent an honest, reliable boy, whom I had, with the articles I had found to the addresses which were given. In the evening he came back radiant with joy. The loser of the letter, in which perhaps a bill of exchange may have been, presented him with a whole guinea. The happy owner of each of the other articles which had been taken back, had likewise given a reward. I was obliged to claim this money for myself; I was obliged to do so, because my money-chest was too far exhausted to meet the reward which I myself, in expectation that I might be fortunate enough to recover my incalculably valuable paper from some honest finder, had placed upon it. This paper could be of no more use to any other person than the building estimates, for which my boy had received a whole crown, were to me. But no such happiness was to fall to my share. However, as I was of the firm opinion and was strengthened in it by my wife, that the important document which we had lost must be lying rolled up, insignificant-looking, dirty, like a piece of old waste paper in some corner of Drury Lane, on some heap of rubbish, at some door, or by some of the kerbstones for preventing the wheels of carriages from inconveniencing foot-passengers, and as night was the only time for prosecuting such searches quietly in London and for picking up every piece of paper lying about, I went out with a hand-lantern and, wonderful result! thus is our life made up! we seek and seek for some ardently desired object, we never attain it but we discover others! We seek the omnipotent power of Providence and we find—His love! We seek eternal truth of thought, and the further it recedes from us and the dimmer the distant view of it becomes, so much the clearer on another side does one star after another sparkle near us; perhaps the star of virtue, perhaps the jewel of true knowledge, which tells us that all we had sought is not so valuable as that which we have found. We have found a keener perception, the improvement of our mind, the taming and controlling of our heart and its desires."

John Robertson now availed himself of the permission of the judge, ceased speaking and rested himself for a few moments on the seat which had been placed for him. When he had revived again, he smiled. It was not so much the pause which had given him fresh strength as the consciousness, from the emotion and sympathy of all his hearers, of the powerful effect of the defence he had made for himself.

"During the next days," he continued, "I did not find what I sought but I found little treasures, so to speak; some beauty had perhaps been talking to a man who was paying her attention and when they parted, neither perceived what she had lost in her absence of mind. Then, in places which our beaux frequent for play, there, where the rich nabob from the Indies banquets, in the neighbourhood of coffee-houses where people are wont to dispute until late at night, I found embroidered handkerchiefs, with initials on which perhaps the owners set a still greater value; I found silver sword tassels and fur trimmings which had dropped unperceived. In churches where evening service was held, such as in Mary-le-bone, I found ornaments of as great value as though the ladies who had come to pray at church had been going to a ball. Oh! how often at night did I hum. on my wanderings, the old song from the lively farce "The Fair of Life;"—

"Old clothes and old rubbish, ah! here you all go!
   For good luck, far from me, you've my prayers;
 A moth-eaten, mouldy lot, many say no,
   Many all the while wish you were theirs."

"There are pretty things here will ne'er give you a wound,
   You may finger at that thing and this;
 Give it me, the old chapman, here every year round,
   And I'll pack it up in a trice."

"The poor and the poorest are guests at our fair,
'Tis a right merry time, an you will;
So they stay till the booths are pulled down to a pair,
And of fun they have all had their fill."

Tears must indeed have been shed in the circle of hearers, for on all sides were audible those stifling noises, that use of the pocket-handkerchief with which men are accustomed to endeavour to conceal their emotion. The tone, rather cheerful than solemn, in which John Robertson recited this poor rag-collector's song, excited among many of his hearers feelings the most contradictory to the emotions which filled all hearts; it excited smiles. For the character of man is to struggle vigorously against giving expression to his inner and better feelings. Men laughed that they might not be obliged to weep.

The accused told of his acquaintance with Will Mordaunt to whom, when things went on worse and worse and he was obliged to be declared bankrupt, he made over his excellent servant on, condition of being able sometimes to employ the latter for his private errands. In this manner, Will Mordaunt became acquainted with Robertson's secret which consisted in nothing but what was the natural consequence of those searchings which the prisoner had described; searchings which were at first merely the result of one fixed idea. The first rounds of the nocturnal wanderer had immediately been attended with such striking success that the sum which Robertson would willingly have paid to the finder of the article he had himself lost was already far exceeded. Speculations, he must above all things give up; proscribed as a bankrupt, he was obliged to retire; no one would give him credit, no undertaking which he began prospered. The only thing which brought in a return, was his nightly wandering begun at first in hope, continued in despair and at last crowned and cheered by astonishing profits.

He had found papers, he said, which belonged to the East India Company and were of the greatest importance. He could not himself give up these papers, because an inquiry would have necessitated his personal appearance in a court of justice; for a charge of fraud had, at first, been made against one of their principal officials. Will Mordaunt undertook to return them to the East India House himself, received the large reward which had been put upon them and was honourable enough to be satisfied with the share which, in such cases, Robertson had arranged according to a fixed tariff. By this means, in Robertson's grateful mind, a feeling of obligation to old Mordaunt was still further strengthened. These strangely fortunate events occurred again and again; there was a regular ledger kept for the accounts between the honourable finder and the man who gave back their property to the persons fortunate enough thus to recover it. Honesty was the first condition in the partnership, which lasted for almost a generation, between Robertson and the miser whose grandson was now a dean and who was among the audience but who kept himself concealed on account of certain embarrassments into which sundry unfinished law-suits of his grandfather might have brought him. The accused concluded his speech with these words,

"I can myself say, and God is my witness, that I have spread abroad much joy and gladness among my fellow-men. From my tears, from the grief of my early lost wife, have sprung for others hours of relief from mourning and repentance. How many a man who staggered through the streets in senseless intoxication lost half his fortune! He vowed to heaven, if he recovered it, to improve and to make the kindness of fortune an incentive to reform. This raised my courage, this rewarded me for the exertions which caused a change in my whole manner of life. It is true, I have often, on one single night, at some place where a great banquet was given or at Vauxhall where thousands were assembled, through the carelessness and incautiousness of people, the want of faithfulness in servants and other causes which those belonging to us do not consider, obtained returns which even a flourishing trade could not have brought in. When I had raised myself again in the world, the profits of my savings helped me forward. But my best reward lay in the feeling that I had worked in the ways of Providence and could say to myself, 'You must have been plunged into darkness and despair that you might find the way to lead yourself and others to the light.' All that I could not restore to its rightful owner, I sent through Will Mordaunt to the police. Many trifles, many insignificant things scarcely worth preserving, have remained in my house and its outbuilding for years. I have often thought that the time would come for these also. For who can tell what is of value to others? The last blessing from the hand of a dying mother may rest on a little book, a little picture which, if advertised as found, could only raise a smile."

The adventures which Robertson had had with Sam Mordaunt, his daughter's betrothed lover, the true disposition of the latter, the marriage with Lord Arthur Maxwell had already been spoken of, without reserve, by his solicitor. Robertson's self-accusation of having behaved dishonourably, for the first time in his life, on finding the courier's pouch was dismissed by the jury upon his offer to compensate the horseman appropriately for the punishment he had undergone and in such a manner as he might choose. Thought and mirth were both excited by the lawyer's description of the sign over the dwelling of his client, the Flying Horse, and of its connection with the attainment of the object of his life. At length the patriotic spirit which he had always shown spoke in favour of the honest man. Once before, he confessed, he had scarcely been able to withstand the temptation not to return something which he had found. It was the bracelet which belonged to Blanche de Champfleury who had disappeared and had without doubt escaped to France. This he had found after a party of disguised persons had passed him about midnight, conversing in French and, as he clearly distinguished, in a highly treasonable manner. Immediately after these men had gone by, he perceived the valuable trinket. Was there then a woman amongst them? He had seen none. It must then have been a lady of rank in disguise. In this case, his supposition that he was on the track of conspirators was all the better founded. As a preliminary measure he gave a hint to the police, without mentioning his name. Hence, the watchmen whom Sam had seen in the autumn in Budge Road. Time, however, was taken by the magistrate in coming to a decision and making any further discoveries till at length, in the autumn Robertson repaired his error and sent the bracelet to the house of Lady Radcliffe, the unfortunate mother of young Lord Derwentwater, recently executed.

Robertson was free. The court rose. Many persons who were quite strangers to him shook him by the hand. His old acquaintances also came forward timidly and sought, in the difficulties of present circumstances and the mixture of political suspicion, to excuse their disowning of a man of whose dinners and wines they had partaken with such pleasure. Robertson bore enmity against no one. He shook the sexton by the hand and said,

"I shall soon come to you to look for my little plot of ground. I should have liked a place kept open by the side of Mary Wilson, but now that must be already tenanted."

Indeed he broke down, deeply moved, when the barrister took his arm, led him down the steps of the court and accompanied him to his carriage. The faithful legal adviser was not a little alarmed when the old man, who had dressed himself entirely in black, lay unconscious at his side in one corner of the carriage and looked as colourless as though he would never again return to life. But, by degrees, he opened his eyes, and by the time they reached the Hall of the silk-mercers' guild, in which Robertson had awaited his trial as a prisoner, he had recovered himself. The citizens of London were, according to their trades, divided into several guilds, which also, to a certain degree, afforded a refuge for their members when amenable to the law. As a man who had been bankrupt, John Robertson found it difficult to obtain admission into a guild; that of the merchants remained inaccessible to him; also that of the conceited cloth-weavers. The silk-mercers' guild was more lenient. They had on their list many French and Walloon refugees.

Robertson's lawyer now made a confession to him. He had written to Lady Maxwell and told her of the position of her father; she might arrive at any moment. This intelligence affected the old man to such a degree that he had not strength sufficient to return at present to the Flying Horse; he said that, for this night at least, he would remain at the sick-mercers' guild. What were his feelings when on awaking the following morning from a deep sleep which had strengthened him, he heard a sweet, soft female voice in the neighbouring room and could say to himself, "Yes it is she, it is my child!"

He got up and dressed himself quickly, so far as was necessary. He made a rattling with the basin which he used for washing; he knew for certain that if it were Ellinor ("and assuredly," he said to himself, "it can be no other"), this affectionate daughter would avoid to overpower him by yielding vehemently to her feelings. But he made such a noise in moving about, he shuffled about so audibly in the slippers which she herself had made, that nothing less could happen than for a gentle knock to make itself heard and a voice to whisper, "Sir, do you then know who—," but he had already opened the door and his child threw herself into his arms.

Lady Maxwell had come from Paris as if on wings. The non-arrival of communications from London, the cessation of the letters, formerly so regularly received, had filled her with alarm. Even before she had received the barrister's second letter, sent after he had prepared her by a first, before the full truth respecting her father had been told her, she had already started, accompanied as far as Calais by her husband who durst not follow her to England. Thanks to the means which Robertson had bestowed upon his child, she was able to travel in a manner suited to her rank.

True, she looked pale with grief and alarm, but she was handsomer and more fully developed in figure than ever and had quite the appearance of a matron. With filial affection and care, she took her father back to the old house in Cavendish Street; ornamented this as in former days; watched, as formerly, over his unpretending life. She was now obliged to check the crowds of people who sought to make acquaintance with the remarkable person, who was everywhere named, "the honest finder." The proud Duchesses of Cleveland and Bolton, who had exerted so much influence with the king and ministers for the pardon and freedom of the prisoners in the Tower, embraced Lady Ellinor Maxwell as their equal, and arranged for the father, the preserver of his son-in-law, an ovation which even Robertson, mindful of his unaltered political opinions, felt obliged to deprecate.

That is, indeed, a painful separation, the separation of a wife from a loved husband, to whom she has been lately married. A German popular proverb represents this position as a semi-widowhood. Certainly Ellinor felt herself like a widow in her solitary state. It was true that she reposed again on the downy couch, on which she had been accustomed formerly to rest (for her father had left the third floor of the house just as it had always been), but the trial became ever greater and greater. For Lord Maxwell's pardon was not to be thought of. Thus the months of separation dragged themselves along, till at last a year had past. Ellinor could not leave her father, whose strength was gradually but certainly ebbing away. Nor could she deprive him of the happiness, the cheering excitement of dandling his little grandchild on his knees, a noble, handsome boy, the perfect image of his father.

A tender and affectionate couple blessed by a child, whom the father has never yet seen, form a sadly touching yet beautiful picture. Neither had anything as consolation, but the exchange of letters. These letters were the utterances of two pure minds, such as approach nearest to that true image of God, who once created this fair and beautiful world and man as its master, nearest to the image of eternal love, Bound firmly together by true love they waited on, separated only by the fulfilment of a noble duty, looking forward full of hope to a reunion, and already rewarded with a child, each smallest particular of whose improvement Ellinor must detail to his father; how many meals he had in the day, what were the first articulate words he uttered, what gave him most pleasure, whether a horse, or a flower, or a kitten on the roof. A mother's heart which, knowing that every word will be received with love, tells and describes everything connected with her child, is the best painter in the world.

At length that party in Parliament was successful which wished to see the rents in English society repaired, the wounds healed which England herself had inflicted. Richard Steele's fiery eloquence and his able pen were urged on by the generous feelings of his heart. Even one of the ministers, Lord Stanhope, was compelled to endeavour to bring an example of inconsistency, which he had himself set, into accordance with the universal mode of procedure against the Jacobite rising. In Maxwell's uncle, Lord Nairn, he had extended mercy to an old school-friend. Lady Nairn, rescued from a fearful fate, treated Ellinor like a daughter. Robert Walpole could now no longer make any opposition. Lord Widdrington, Earl Carnwarth were pardoned. A universal amnesty permitted the proscribed, and some of those, who were condemned to death, to return to England under certain conditions.

It was not until after three years of most painful separation, that Lord Maxwell was reunited to his wife and saw his handsome boy for the first time. The child was frightened at his father, who seized on him and would have kissed and caressed him. It was not until the child saw that his father and mother were weeping (both were dressed in mourning), that he advanced to his kind father, as though wishing to comfort him. Then, when bound together by embraces and caresses, they drove outside the gates of London to the new church-yard of St. Paul's.

For there Ellinor had laid her father only a few weeks previously. The old man's eyes had not been able to bear the fulness of light which, after so long a night of darkness, had burst in upon him in the reunion with his son-in-law. Mr. Wetherby had devised means to comply with his wishes. He was resting by the side of Mary Wilson, his wife.

THE END.

PRINTING OFFICE OF THE PUBLISHER.

www.ingramcontent.com/pod-product-compliance
Lightning Source LLC
Chambersburg PA
CBHW030751230426
43667CB00007B/921